# *Marjorie*

## *An ordinary woman with an extraordinary gift*

*by*

*Paul Williamson*

Published by Soul Light Publishing

*Marjorie – an ordinary woman with an extraordinary gift*

TABLE OF CONTENTS

# Foreword

## *A Profile of Marjorie*

Marjorie Wilson was a very inspiring and competent Spiritual channel. She died in June 2004, having just celebrated her seventieth birthday. Marjorie's life stemmed from a modest working class background. In her personality, she was unremarkable, for she regarded herself as a very ordinary person who did not have a lot of confidence in herself. During her young life, she worked as a secretary, and married Reg, who was then a professional ice skater. From her earliest days, she had an undying love for the theatre, an interest she shared with her sister, Joan, and best friend, Ruth. In the last twenty-five years of her life, she suffered great pain and progressive physical impairment from Rheumatoid Arthritis, an illness that increasingly ravaged her body.

It was only in her final fourteen years that I became associated with Marjorie. She was very frail and weak, struggling to keep going. But she had a sparkle in her eyes, and warmth about her that showed she was interested and cared about humanity. She had a strong will and strived to express herself fully, impulses that were eroded, sadly, by her illness.

In working with me, she discovered that she had a great capacity within her to develop Spiritual awareness. Central to this was the discovery she made that she had a personal guide working with her. His name was Sojah (pronounced 'Sawyer'). Accessing Sojah changed her life and gave depth and purpose to her life that had not been there before.

Marjorie could go into a deep state of trance and allow Sojah to speak through her. When she channeled Sojah, her voice and manner changed. From that state of trance, Marjorie's head would rise up from her chest, and it would be Sojah, not Marjorie, that spoke. Marjorie would be sleeping while Sojah was present. Sojah's personality was very different from her own, an upright male presence, full of dignity and wisdom. It was Sojah's mission to spread teachings about Spiritual life and encourage people to seek guidance from Spiritual sources, something he felt that our society needed desperately, as a means to bring more love into our world.

Sojah was an entity that inspired and moved people. He could be as much humble as he could knowledgeable. To various audiences, he gave discourses on many topics of which Marjorie was ignorant. Numerous people, including myself, had their outlooks to life changed by what he taught. He described the Spiritual worlds to us and helped us to connect with our Spiritual guides, emphasizing the need for us to be loving in our actions and respectful to others.

For those who were privileged enough to witness Marjorie channelling Sojah, there was much to learn and appreciate. People who listened were drawn to Sojah like a magnet, although it was only a comparative few who were exposed to Sojah's teachings during Marjorie's lifetime.

In channeling Sojah, Marjorie was utterly selfless in offering herself to do this, even at times when she was suffering acutely and not coping with her own condition. For her, it was an act of service that she felt she had to do, because she felt it was right. There was little benefit that she gained from this work for herself, apart from the feeling of joy that she could be helping others.

Usually when Marjorie channeled Sojah, she would be completely unconscious with no memory of what happened afterwards. It was only through listening to tapes of the sessions with Sojah, that she could acquaint herself with what he taught. All she would feel would be the love generated by Sojah as he spoke to others through her. Sometimes she would listen afterwards to the tapes of her sessions of channeling Sojah in amazement, marvelling at the words that had been spoken with her voice.

Marjorie had her own relationship with Sojah and he tried to help her with her problems, as well as offer her peace and inner comfort. Marjorie had to go through her own process of how much she could accept of Sojah's suggestions and then decide to what extent she would act on them. In this, Marjorie was very human, feeling doubtful and skeptical. She even turned away from the help that Sojah offered her at times.

Marjorie could channel other beings beside Sojah, including Dagmar, who is a healing guide associated with me. Dagmar channeled teachings about Spiritual healing that also inspired many people to try this and bring healing to others.

Much has been documented of Sojah's teachings and the main essence of his wisdom was conveyed in my first book, 'Healing Journeys'. However, there is much more to Sojah than could be expressed there, so it is hoped that this book will perform that task more fully.

The first part of this book will outline the story of Marjorie's life and death and her evolution into Spirit. It begins with details of her early life and circumstances that led to her becoming a Spiritual channel, and all the change and adjustments that this brought to her. It will show Marjorie's compassion but also her mistakes, her fears and her despair that she was not a perfect person, but rather someone with much to learn who tried her best in a very difficult situation. Following this will be the story of Marjorie's death and what people perceived of her journey into Spirit. There are also chapters about my own contact with Marjorie and Sojah in Spirit, after her death, and what I sensed they channeled to me.

The second part of the book will be devoted to a comprehensive outline of

Sojah's teachings. Although there is a large legacy of transcribed material from numerous sessions with Sojah, I have chosen in this book to express my own interpretation of the essence of his teachings. It is possible that some of my own thoughts have merged with Sojah's outlook, in what I have written. I acknowledge that. The main reason that I have taken this approach has been to preserve a continuity of writing style throughout the book. Every effort has been made to ensure the integrity of what Sojah wished to convey. Some of the subjects explored include descriptions of the Spiritual planes, astral travel and practical advice about developing a Spiritual outlook.

At the end of our healing evenings, Sojah used to channel meditations that would aim to lift our consciousness out of our bodies and take us on an inner journey to the Spiritual realm nearest our own, the plane where we all go when we die. He called this beautiful plane, as others have done, the Summerland. Some of these meditations are included at the end of this book and have been written in a form where readers could practice these at home. A CD, of Sojah's meditations, is being prepared, as an accompaniment to this volume.

Sojah expressed many times that he wished for his teachings to be spread as far and wide as possible. This book represents an attempt for this to be accomplished. Integral to appreciating Sojah, is the story of Marjorie, her human frailties, the role of suffering in her life, and how she fared with the Spiritual purpose of being a channel for Sojah. Marjorie's personality contrasts so markedly with that of Sojah, with his assurance, insight and love. But their cooperation was very strong and their bond very loving. It demanded a joint effort for them to accomplish what they did.

People might find that discussion of issues in this book, such as questions of how to deal with personal suffering and live a worthwhile life in a challenging world, could inspire. Marjorie's life suggests that there can be Spiritual meaning underlying all that we experience and that it is important for us to persevere and do our best, whatever our circumstances.

# Dedication

This book is about Marjorie, her life, and her gift as a Spiritual channel. However, I would like to acknowledge her husband, Reg, and the huge role that he has played, both in Marjorie's life, and in providing an inspiration for this book.

For a vast period of his adult life, Reg displayed selfless devotion to oversee Marjorie's needs when she was incapacitated. This was so vital in many, many ways to her well-being and involved a great deal of sacrifice on his part. During times when she would descend into despair, he would strive to remain optimistic. When her faith and will to live faltered, his faith would remain steadfast. Even near the end, when they both struggled to cope, mentally and physically, Reg refused to give up on Marjorie, even when she tried to send him away.

In the time since Marjorie's death, Reg has continued to try to live his life constructively, even though he has had his own physical problems. He has spent many hours giving feedback and information to help with this project.

For much of his life, Reg has been an unsung hero, a quiet man in the background. He deserves praise. Sojah once remarked that Reg was quite an evolved soul and cited how Reg was placid and could accept much of the difficulties that life brought to him. His compassion has shone like a bright light. This book is for him more than anyone else.

# *The author's relationship with Marjorie*

Since the early 1980's, I had been leading inner development workshops, and helping people in groups. From that base, I learned to work as a therapist, helping people individually through hypnotherapy and past life regression.

Although much of my relationship with Marjorie was in connection with my work, Marjorie also became a close personal friend. Through the cooperative bond that I shared with Marjorie over many years, I learnt a lot from the Spiritual work that we did together. In relating to Sojah, Marjorie's guide, I could acknowledge a being that impressed me greatly. He was someone who challenged my notions of reality and introduced concepts about the nature of the Spiritual worlds that felt deeply true. People exposed regularly to his presence grew calmer, wiser and more accepting of their lives.

Marjorie was someone I could trust and confide in, a person with whom I felt completely safe to share about my own life issues and problems. With her own difficulties, I could support her too.

Now that she has died, I miss her, but accept that our meeting served its purpose and it is a phase of my life that is now over.

This book is intended as a testimony to her and to the work we did together, especially the Spiritual aspect. It has been written with the hope that the knowledge we gained can be passed on to others.

# *Part 1 – Marjorie's life and death*

## Chapter 1: Marjorie the person

Marjorie was a child of the war. She was born in Murrfield, Yorkshire, in 1934. When she was two, her family moved to Morecambe, where she spent the rest of her childhood. Her parents bought a Guest House and her father worked on the railway. As was typical for that time, her parents were both very busy. While her father was away working, her mother ran the Guest House. There were two other children in the family. Joan was twelve years older than Marjorie and helped her mother in the Guest House. Charles was eight years older, but Marjorie felt that he was a nuisance to him and stayed out of his way most of the time. Consequently, Marjorie was often left to her own devices.

The family was very important to Marjorie, but it was a place where she also felt a lot of pain. It appears that during the times when she was free, that her mother doted on her. When Marjorie was born, her mother moved out of the marriage bed and shared a bedroom with her, rather than staying with her father. Other members of the family felt that she was spoilt, and resented the attention that Marjorie received from her mother. They felt that she gave much less to them. This was especially true of her father.

Marjorie felt that her father rejected her. She adored her father and craved his love, but felt that he gave very little to her. Whenever she went near him, she felt that he turned away. During one stage of her life, Marjorie wondered if he was even her actual father, because he tended to neglect her so much. All the attention she received from her mother was not always what she wanted. She would have preferred if this attention had come from her father. There is an implication that he felt rejected, himself, from Marjorie's mother preferring Marjorie, and the pain of this prevented him from sharing his love with her.

Marjorie's father could be quite cruel to her. The strongest example Marjorie shared with me came from when she was fourteen. Marjorie did some child minding, looking after a little boy. The parents of this boy offered to buy Marjorie a dog for her birthday. This is something that she would have dearly loved. However, later, Marjorie found out that her father had forbidden this boy's parents from giving her this. Marjorie felt that this type of behavior was typical of his attitude towards her. Even though he did do the practical things needed to look after her, she did not feel his support for her or any appreciation for her. She never gave up trying though, but for her whole life, Marjorie failed to come to terms with her father's rejection of her. She felt deeply hurt.

Later, in her work with me, when her parents had been long dead, Marjorie was given the opportunity to meet with her father in Spirit during one of her inner journeys she had, that I facilitated. She felt guided along a path that led to a house in Spirit. Instinctively, she knew that he was waiting there, but as she came near, she became distressed and turned away. She had to come out of the meditation. It was too painful for her to face him.

Marjorie blamed her mother for turning her father against her. To explain why she continued to sleep in the bedroom with Marjorie, her mother told the others in the family that Marjorie did not like the dark, and so she needed her to be there with a night-light to keep her company. In fact, Marjorie was very aware that it was her mother that didn't like the dark and not her. She felt used, but because she was a small child, there was nothing she could say. It was the generation where children were seen but not heard. In addition, her mother gave her anything that she wanted as an attempt to keep her on her side. This made her very unpopular with her brother, sister and father, who did not enjoy the same privileges. So, at times, Marjorie felt a bit of an outcast. She could have everything she demanded from her mother, but what she really wanted was simple love and acceptance from her family, something that eluded her.

Consequently, Marjorie sought emotional bonding from others outside her family. During the war, her parent's house became an RAF refuge and Marjorie gained some satisfaction for her needs with airmen that stayed with them. Each morning, she would come down and see a row of bayonets leant against the wall. They were only very young men, and some of them looked quite scared. There were those who liked little girls and would sit her on their knee and play with her. Some took her out, bought her presents and ice cream. She enjoyed the closeness, but then, every six months, there would be a change over and a new batch of airmen would arrive, so her experience with the airmen was very transitory. This was as much exposure as Marjorie had with the war. In many ways, she was quite fortunate.

While the airmen were coming and going, Marjorie was developing her friendship with an older girl whose name was Ruth. It was the beginning of the war, and Marjorie was only five. Ruth and Marjorie's sister, Joan, were members of a local dramatic society. Ruth was ten at the time and Joan, fourteen. Joan brought Ruth home one day, and immediately, the three of them bonded together very well and became close. They each had needs that the others could fulfil. It felt like a fated meeting. During one conversation, Ruth confided that she had always wanted two sisters. Joan affirmed that God had decreed that she did have two sisters. The three of them laughed about it, but from then on, they were like sisters for the rest of their lives.

Later, as Ruth Holden, Ruth would become quite a famous actress, appearing in Coronation Street and numerous television productions. For Marjorie, I sense that Ruth became more important even than her own sister. They could laugh together, have fun, talk about everything and anything.

Marjorie was in awe of Joan and Ruth. She would follow them around and pretend to know what they were talking about with all the theatre goings-on. Marjorie never once believed that she could be an actress to the same degree as Ruth and Joan. She did not feel that she had the same capability. But she loved to be in their company and share their light, and they in turn, were protective of her and included her in their experiences.

While Joan and Ruth grew up to pursue their interests and careers in the theatre, when Marjorie was old enough, she became a secretary. Her main work was with calculating machines, adding up accounts. She was very skilled at this work, and highly regarded in her work places. This in turn boosted her self-esteem. The only problem she had around her work concerned her deafness.

From her early childhood, Marjorie had had difficulties with her hearing. Perhaps it could have been treated then, because, as she got older, the problem became worse, but in the end, as a young adult, Marjorie had two major operations on her ears. The first operation was damaging and resulted in almost the complete loss of hearing in one of her ears. Then, the hearing in the other ear deteriorated to the point where in one episode, her colleagues at work were shouting out numbers for her to enter on the calculating machine, and she couldn't hear them, so she needed to leave her work. The second operation, to correct degeneration of the mastoid bone, involving taking out the eardrum completely, was remarkably successful and did have a restorative affect upon her hearing, to a degree. Sadly though, she did continue to have trouble with deafness for the rest of her life.

Marjorie only had one serious relationship with a man in her life, and that was with her husband, Reg. Initially, they met while Reg was involved in his work as a professional Ice Skater. He received an invitation to attend the rehearsals of a Musical production nearby to where he was working. Marjorie had a part in this production. It seemed by chance that they met. She was twenty-one and he was two years older. They quickly became good friends and close companions and dated together throughout that summer. But then, Reg's work took him elsewhere and he travelled far and wide. It was a situation they both accepted. They only met on rare and precious occasions but continued to stay in contact with each other. It was only nine years later that their relationship developed more seriously.

Marjorie was almost thirty years old when Reg invited her to come and meet his family and friends. Then, one morning, Marjorie got up, and found a brown envelope in the porch way of the house where she lived. Marjorie thought it was a photograph, but inside, there was a blue box, and in the blue box was an engagement ring. This was Reg's way of proposing. That, morning, Marjorie was so excited and wanting to tell everyone she met, that she forgot to eat her breakfast. In a letter with the ring, Reg asked her to write to him and say whether she would marry him or not. Although she was a little bit coy about it, she did want to marry him really, and was ready to move on in her life.

I sense that they loved each other very dearly and were happy together. There was quite a contrast in their personalities. Although Reg could be a showman with his ice-skating, he was quite a private individual really, and enjoyed his time with Marjorie on his own. Marjorie, on the other hand, was more outgoing, and enjoyed social contact with others. He grew to be very devoted to her, and as she faced more challenges in her life, he typically put his own needs second, to be able to support her.

They wanted to have a family together, and made several attempts. However, Marjorie was not able to carry her pregnancies full term, and had several miscarriages. It was a tragedy in her life not to have children, because she loved children very much. As a substitute to these desires, she became a child minder, and dedicated her heart to looking after children. She formed some very close bonds with the children that she did care for, and they appreciated her very much. It did not remove though, the ache of not having children that were biologically hers.

Worse trials were to come for Marjorie. When she was forty-six years old, she was diagnosed with Rheumatoid Arthritis. Marjorie had been entertaining one of her friends when suddenly she could not move her arm. The next morning, her leg was just as immobile. In the following days, and by resting, Marjorie slowly recovered from this initial disability. Sadly, though, it was just the beginning. When she was given the diagnosis, Marjorie did not realize about the crippling nature of this illness. However, in time, the relentless progression of this horrifying disease gradually twisted and rotted her joints and bones. Over the years, the illness restricted more and more her capacity to do the physical activities she loved.

She tried to fight the condition and not surrender to it, but even though there were times of hope, these turned to despair as her physical being further declined. Eventually, she had operations on her hip, knee and hand, and in her last years, was not even able to feed herself, and was continuously on strong painkillers to cope with the never-ending pain.

What is interesting about this is that Sojah, Marjorie's guide, has spoken many times about how the Rheumatoid arthritis is actually something that Marjorie, as a soul, chose before her life began, as a trial that she would endure. This is quite astonishing, because Marjorie as a personality, with her will, would never have wished to suffer with arthritis at all. She could hardly bear that she was restricted from doing so much that her desires wanted to do. Yet, in a way, the restrictions in her ability to fulfil her physical desires would provide an opportunity for her to turn to God and Spirit and for her inner psychic and Spiritual faculties to grow stronger. When she could not so much use her physical body, then she could apply herself to enable her inner faculties to develop.

So, the arthritis was a Spiritual test that she was giving herself, not a punishment, but an opportunity for her to focus upon Spiritual matters, to learn, and serve. But it was still a matter of choice whether she would do so.

In the early stages, though, Marjorie tried to carry on, and maintain as normal a life as she could, determined to not let the illness defeat her.

It was only a few years after this that Marjorie's sister, Joan, developed Alzheimer's disease. This was a huge shock. Joan was only fifty-nine. She had been living just down the road in Brighton, and the two sisters were in regular contact. Joan started by becoming forgetful, then repeating things, and becoming ever more erratic in her behaviour. It was immensely disturbing for Marjorie to witness her sister's decline. The transformation in Joan's personality, from someone that Marjorie had spent her life admiring and respecting, to a shell of a person that did not even recognize her, was extremely sad and stressful. While she still had some moments of clarity, Joan expressed the wish to return to Morecambe to live, and Marjorie and Reg accompanied her so they could help look after her. For Marjorie, moving from the relatively dry and warmer climate of Brighton to the damp and colder climate of Morecambe, was a disaster for her arthritis. Joan had to be placed in a home where she could receive full time care, and she eventually died there. Meanwhile, Marjorie's physical condition deteriorated rapidly.

Marjorie was feeling increasingly depressed and struggling to find a purpose in being alive. Marjorie's sister, Joan, might have died, but at least she still had her best friend, Ruth. Ruth was very concerned for Marjorie and tried to help her. Ruth was based in Morecambe, so at least the two friends could have more time to enjoy each other's companionship. It was Ruth, who first came across the work that I was doing, and attended one of my Self-Hypnosis classes. She asked if I would come and visit Marjorie. I agreed. The journey for me to visit Marjorie's house meant for me to walk a few hundred metres across the road. It is amazing that we lived so close. Marjorie would acknowledge that meeting me was the key event for her in beginning to do her Spiritual work.

# Chapter 2 - Formative Spiritual influences and experiences

Marjorie's capacity to be a Spiritual channel remained latent until quite late in her life, but she did have some significant experiences that helped to arouse her interest in Spiritual and psychic matters from her teenage years onwards.

As a child, Marjorie was raised to be a Christian, and she attended Church and Sunday School. Her mother would read her stories from the Bible and taught her to pray. She was indoctrinated with the belief that God was all-powerful and would take note of all the good and bad things that she did. When she did good things then God would love her. When she did things that displeased God, he would not stop loving her, but he would be very sad. Marjorie did have a faith and believed in God, but playing out with her friends was more important to her.

After the war, Marjorie's parents bought a shop that they ran. Marjorie had to sleep in the room at the top of the house. She was eleven when they moved there. From the beginning, Marjorie felt disturbed in this room as if there was the psychic presence of someone that did not want her there. Over the years, when she was sleeping, Marjorie had various nightmares about being strangled and rope placed around her neck. There were times when she woke up and the light would be on when she knew that she had turned it off. The door would shut and there would be nobody there. Marjorie tried to laugh these things off.

Once, she woke up and there seemed to be two shapes at the base of her bed, one was a bit taller than the other. She put her head under the bedcovers so that she would not see them. Another time, she woke up and there appeared to be someone dragging their foot around the room. She perceived there to be two beds, and sometimes, on the other bed, there was somebody lying there. Marjorie questioned herself whether it might be her imagination, but when the light came on and off while she was watching, with no one there, she knew it was real. And it never stopped.

Marjorie tried to tell her family about the phenomena in the room, but her father in particular, dismissed them. Finally, when they left that house and bought another one, Marjorie was told by her brother that the room where she had slept had the reputation for being haunted. For all these years, the rest of her family had known this but had kept it secret. They couldn't sell the house because they depended on it for their livelihood.

Later, Ruth relayed to Marjorie a story she had heard from her elderly Aunt. Apparently, some years earlier, her aunt had been with a group of people walking up the street from the church when they had looked up to the top window of the shop, and saw a dead youth whose body was hanging there with a rope tied around his neck.

Usually when people die, their consciousness leaves the physical body and rises up into the light where it is integrated into the Spiritual realm of being. Sometimes, souls choose not to do this, and remain close to the place where their body died, especially if they have some strong emotional attachment to the body they left. It is likely that the consciousness of this teenage boy was still lingering around the room where he had lived as an Earth Bound Spirit and that Marjorie picked up the impressions of this. Although the experiences relating to this were disturbing to Marjorie, they probably did help to activate her psychic faculties, and they stimulated her interest in the paranormal, thus serving a purpose in Marjorie's development.

There was much suspicion within the church of her upbringing about people experimenting with the 'occult', but this did not stop Marjorie's friend, Ruth from using the ouji board. But inviting Spirits to come forward by this means was not a very safe practice, and Ruth became rather scared when forces seemed to be moving her hands and operating beyond the board beyond her control.

The next major Spiritual experience for Marjorie happened when she went deaf. Having to leave her work because of deafness was enormously frustrating for her. She felt in despair and did not know where to turn. Marjorie felt drawn to go to the local library and was most attracted to the section about Spiritual and psychic matters.

One of the books she read was by the famous healer, Harry Edwards. She felt inspired to write to him, describe her condition and ask if he could send her healing. In the reply that she received, she was instructed to write back every week giving feedback about what was happening with her hearing and any unusual experiences that she had. Marjorie did as was suggested, and immediately, she noticed strange things that began to happen.

One evening, she woke up and thought she could see someone's spiritual form standing by her bed. On another occasion, she felt her father's presence, even though he was living in the other end of the country, in Morecambe. Then, finally, in the middle of one night, Marjorie woke up with a loud crackling in both ears. The next morning, she went to the hairdressers wearing her hearing aid. Taking this off, it dawned on her that she could hear what people were saying, and a radio was playing low, something that she did not normally hear. It was all rather alarming, and she felt suddenly frightened. Going home from the hairdressers, she tested her hearing by knocking on things and could hardly believe it that sounds came to her so loud and clear.

This activation of her hearing capacity lasted about ten days before it started to diminish again. The most astonishing thing was that it was through her left ear that she could hear most. This was the ear that had been damaged by the earlier operation, so according to the consultant, she shouldn't be hearing from that ear at all.

Marjorie argued with the consultant about this, and it was with her insistence that he finally agreed to do the operation that did help to restore her hearing to an extent.

The healing was remarkable. It appeared that Harry Edwards had visited Marjorie in his psychic body, and with his Spirit helpers, had performed an energy operation upon her ears. The fact that he could do this and gain a dramatic physical result – i.e. the temporary restoration of her hearing, helped enormously to develop Marjorie's faith in the capacity of Spirit.

A further instance of Marjorie receiving healing occurred in the early stages, after Marjorie had been diagnosed with Rheumatoid Arthritis. At this time, her feet had become weak and were difficult to walk on and she suffered a lot of pain in her back.

One day, as she hobbled along the street, a small lady approached her and explained that she was a healer, and offered to help. She came around to Marjorie's place, took off her scarf, warmed her hands, and then placed her hands on Marjorie's body. While the lady was touching her, Marjorie could feel no pain. It was very relaxing. The small lady would chat away about her life and work as a healer seemingly without making any effort with regards to the healing that she was doing. She did not want any money, and offered to come regularly on a Monday, which is what happened.

At first Marjorie doubted that there would be any improvement, but soon her pain eased, and people noticed how much more freely Marjorie seemed to be walking. Marjorie was very enthusiastic about the healing that she received and the small lady received lots of referrals from people with whom Marjorie talked. This was another example of Spirit coming to help her at a time when she really needed it, and as a prompt for her to strengthen her faith. From the way Marjorie described it, I do not think that she fully realized the impact that the healing was having upon her to make her feel better. It was the time when her sister Joan was becoming ill, and when Marjorie moved house to go and live in Morecambe, the healing was interrupted. Marjorie did not expect her condition to alter, but it did, and worsened considerably after a short space of time. It was a difficult time for Marjorie, and she was obviously very occupied with the deteriorating condition of her sister. Marjorie put the change in her own state of health more down to the damp climate, and she was not able to find any more healing help in this new locality where she lived.

Marjorie continued to have some degree of interest in Spiritual matters. She had a questioning mind and was an avid reader with wide ranging interests. On the Spiritual front, she was drawn more towards reading books by mediums such as Doris Stokes and others.

Marjorie did have a feeling that there was someone in Spirit watching over her. She did not try to define it. It was just a knowing that she was not alone with what she did. There is the story related in 'Healing Journeys', where she was about to get into her bath, and she heard a loud shout of 'no' inside her mind. Fortunately, she listened to what the voice told her, for a glass object had broken and left sharp slivers of glass in the bath where Marjorie was about to sit.

Stemming from her teenage years, Marjorie was aware of the power of Spiritual reality, and she could be rather afraid of psychic matters, but she was also intensely interested. What she needed was a sense of understanding so that it would feel safe for her to explore this.

When I first met Marjorie, she wanted to discuss my views of the afterlife. She was fascinated with the idea that it could be possible to contact the Spirits of dead relatives who had passed over, as a proof of survival after death. But the concept that we all had a loving Spiritual guide, from a higher dimension of reality, supporting us and protecting us, was not a concept that she had dwelled upon.

The occasion, when she first encountered her Spiritual guide, Sojah, while on an inner meditative journey in one of our therapy sessions, must have been a huge surprise for her.

# Chapter 3: Marjorie – the Spiritual channel

I found Marjorie to be a very receptive subject for hypnosis. When I used a standard induction, Marjorie's body would gradually slump and she would become very relaxed. Her inner perceptions would open, and she would become very absorbed in the experiences of her inner world. She would hear my voice and respond to that but all other details of her normal world, including awareness of the discomforts in her physical body, would disappear.

For Marjorie, to go into hypnosis, was a relief. It was a welcome escape from the misery and continual pain and discomfort that she felt in her physical body. The only difficult part was when she had to return and reawaken to the restrictions of her normal world.

Marjorie had expressed the interest in exploring her past lives, and we did that. She would see visions, and feel the emotions of the past life personality she was accessing, very vividly. As I watched her, there were times when her face would light up with happiness, and other moments when she would crumple and cry. She lived these past lives as if they were happening right now.

The part she liked the best, was when the past life character she was channelling died and she could experience leaving the body and ascending up into Spirit. The feeling of love and the Spiritual light was extremely real to her, and she was drawn to want to explore the Spirit world, like a magnet.

Even though she was such a good subject for inner exploration, and she became so absorbed in her experiences, she could still use the capacity of her will. If she did not want to do something that I suggested to her, she could refuse to go there. If she liked somewhere and wished to be there, then she could override my suggestions to do what she wanted. We sometimes needed to negotiate, and Marjorie did basically respect what I was doing with her, and how I wished to lead her process, so we rarely had any conflict. I also felt the need to cooperate with her inner wishes, and was interested what she could learn by her following these.

My own interest was in the past lives, and I wanted to trace any inner patterns that might be contributing to the arthritis. Marjorie wanted to explore and learn about being in the Spirit world. She felt very much at home there. More and more, that is what we did.

Marjorie's face was full of wonder while she visited the Spirit world. She marvelled at the space and vastness of this realm and had spectacular visions of loving Spiritual beings in robes and natural settings like waterfalls and healing temples. At times, she would look radiant with joy at the visions she was having, and afterwards would engage in earnest conversations reflecting about it.

For someone whose physical world was collapsing, these inner explorations gave her a vibrant new interest to pursue.

Very often, Marjorie would travel to a familiar meadow as a first step in her exploration of the Spiritual worlds. This was no ordinary meadow. All her senses were roused to an extraordinary degree when she visited this meadow. The colour of the grass was an incredibly rich green, the scent of the flowers was very strong and aromatic, and the ground beneath her had an energy about it that was animated and alive. While in this meadow, Marjorie could be aware of herself running and feeling free. She could direct herself as she willed. This was quite amazing for her, considering the physical limitations that she faced in her everyday life.

In any of the explorations we did at this time, Marjorie would adjust her perceptions to the meadow first, and then she would be ready to expand her awareness further to other Spiritual places that she could visit.

The way in which Marjorie described her experiences was so immediate, and affecting for her, that there was no thought in my own mind that she was creating this in her normal imagination. True, the experiences were channeling themselves through her imaginative faculty, but not in a way where she was constructing their details first. It was only afterwards that her analytical mind would strive to come to terms with what she had experienced. Marjorie, in her consciousness, was somehow removed from her physical body with her explorations, even though her body registered what happened. It was a mode of perception where experiences presented themselves to her consciousness, and as she accepted them, they unfolded further. By welcoming what came to her and surrendering to this, her sensory awareness opened up to beauty and love of the Spiritual realm. Her normal consciousness had to adjust to this because the impressions she gained in the Spiritual realm were more subtle and finer in their vibration than what she was used to in the physical body. It was a much more powerful form of love energy that she was now experiencing directly.

I believe that on the level of soul, that Marjorie had been prepared, so that when the time came for her to do this, she was able to open herself to these perceptions without causing damage to herself. Exploring the Spiritual world felt like being home for her, and therefore, the process worked smoothly and gracefully.

One day, when she visited the meadow, I asked Marjorie if she was aware of any wise Spiritual beings that were with her and could help her. At first, she didn't understand what I meant, and replied that she didn't see anybody. But then, very suddenly, a very serene, loving presence appeared before her. In her vision, he appeared as an older man, wearing a Roman Toga, being very distinguished and dignified. He spoke to her in her mind and told her that his name was Sojah, and that he was her personal Spiritual guide. Sojah explained that, as a being, he had moved beyond the need of physical incarnation, and that now he was residing on the seventh Spiritual plane of existence. To meet her, Sojah had descended to a level where Marjorie could perceive him. In essence, he was energetically a being of light and love and that he had taken on the form that Marjorie saw so that she could recognize him. Before Marjorie had been born, Sojah had been assigned to her to protect her soul and support her on her Spiritual path. He knew her soul and its limitations and potentials for learning more intimately than anyone else. His task was to encourage her to make steps in her life to move forward as a soul, while being mindful that she needed to make her own decisions and that he could only help her when she asked for it. Sojah assured Marjorie that he had been close by and with her during every step of her life, and that he had been waiting patiently for this moment when they could finally meet consciously together.

Sojah then told Marjorie that he was also a Spiritual teacher, and that their meeting together had been planned. He had come to her, not only to help her, but also for others. Sojah wanted to teach about Spirit and Spiritual life, and that for people to become more aware of these matters, could help them on their own Spiritual journeys.

At the end of this session, Sojah told Marjorie that she only needed to think of him and that he would be there for her. He suggested that it would be useful to have some further sessions where he could talk and begin to explain his teachings to us. Sojah told us that it was healthy and important to challenge any inner experiences that we had, but that he was real and he did exist as a being independent of Marjorie, and was there to help.

Marjorie was very taken aback by the depth of love she felt from Sojah. He felt very familiar to her, and she felt that he was the one that had been there in the background, right through the course of her life. With Sojah, she felt no fear, only trust and love. Meeting Sojah for the first time brought a deep feeling of calm to her that was very healing. For Marjorie, her exchanges with Sojah were a very personal experience. She could not convey easily what she perceived with him, because it was not Earthly. The quality of love that she felt coming from Sojah could only be fully felt by her, but she felt that it was stronger than any love that she could produce, a stronger energy than she had. This convinced her that his presence was something beyond her. It felt that there was somebody there that genuinely cared and knew every aspect of her.

In subsequent sessions, Sojah began to outline the fundamentals of his Spiritual teachings to us. He explained that although he had earned the right to live on the seventh Spiritual plane of existence, that there were many beings higher than he was. Ultimately, all Spiritual beings aspired to become pure beings of love and light, expressing what may be termed the will of 'God'.

As human souls, we had been created to learn the lessons of love and gain experience of life. We lived through various lifetimes, reincarnating to face trials and challenges in order for us to learn. As we learned our lessons, we could gain maturity in our soul and advance higher in the planes of existence. Our souls resided not so much in the physical plane of earthly existence, but in the Spiritual planes, and this was where we felt most at home.

Sojah told us that he had lived many lifetimes on earth, and during his time, had made many mistakes, even one lifetime that he remembered where he brought a lot of suffering upon others. Eventually though, he had learnt his lessons sufficiently so that he did not need to incarnate anymore. One of his last incarnations on earth had been from the Roman times. This had been a happy life and this was why he chose to appear in this form to Marjorie. The memory of this lifetime was very dear to him.

Our lives on earth could be very difficult, but all our experiences had a purpose and could be learning opportunities for us. When we faced a trial in our lives, it was generally better for us to accept this rather than try to fight it or resist it by attempting to avoid it. If we did not know what to do, we could inwardly ask for help from our Spiritual guides, from 'God', or whatever spiritual power we felt could help us. We needed to practice love and kindness in our lives along the lines of treating others in the way that we would like to be treated ourselves.

People on earth all had a Spiritual guide assigned to them. Our guides would be with us from a time before we were born through to after we died. They would assist us to make a plan of learning for us of what we hoped to achieve during our lifetime. Then after our physical bodies died, they would support us to review what we had achieved during the life that we had lived. During the course of the life, they would protect us and prompt us, if we were open for help, so that we would remain true to the path that we had chosen. The link between a guide and their one on Earth was very intimate and personal, and there was a learning process both for the guide as well as the one on earth.

Sojah told Marjorie that he was with her to teach as well as be her personal guide, and that this was something that they had both chosen. As they fulfilled this purpose, it would help both of them to grow and move higher.

It was suggested that a special effort was being made at this time by beings in Spirit so that the divide between the Spiritual realms and earthly experience could be lessened so that more Spiritual love could permeate human cultures on Earth and make our world a happier place to live in. There were concerns that if this did not happen, then there could be much suffering and destruction on our planet in the coming times.

Our earth was only one of many places where life existed, and with our free wills and our tendency towards greed and selfishness, we had a choice whether we would eventually destroy our world or whether we could achieve a spiritual wholeness and evolve spiritually as a race.

Marjorie was fascinated by what Sojah had to say. She sensed his words as thoughts coming into her head and she would relay them aloud to me. While she was communicating this, she would be aware of his presence as a vision standing in front of her. Sojah would correct Marjorie if she did not convey some concept or line of thoughts accurately. In these early stages, Marjorie liked to intervene and ask her own questions as part of our process, so we could have three way conversations going on.

Much of what Sojah had to say was new to Marjorie, and his teachings had a big impact on her outlook to life. Her husband, Reg, was also a witness to all the sessions, and they were both ready to embrace the Spiritual teachings that Sojah imparted. Marjorie felt that she was being asked to serve Sojah, and from her contact with him, she felt the utmost reverence and respect for his work with her.

Soon Sojah asked, for his conversations with me, if he could move closer to Marjorie, and overshadow her with his consciousness, even moving her consciousness away from her physical body, so that he could have the space to speak more directly through her mind. Sojah wanted to train Marjorie to become a Spiritual channel. She was willing to do this, and it was a gradual process of adjustment and experimentation. For Marjorie, this was an act of Spiritual service and the outcome of it meant that she would no longer participate in the conversations I had with Sojah. She would not be there. What she would sense would be a wonderful feeling of peace as she returned to her body at the end of a session, and she felt comfortable to do it.

To assist Marjorie, we often taped sessions with Sojah or made detailed notes, so that Marjorie could refer to these later. Although this was a sacrifice for Marjorie, she also felt pride that she could be used for something that was useful and good. Talking to me was really just a preparation for Sojah to channel through Marjorie to reach much larger groups of people. Sojah told us that we would have our own Healing Circle, that I would be writing books on the subject, and that we would be doing a great deal of Spiritual work in service to others.

Each session with Sojah was different and would offer something new. I would guide Marjorie into the trance state and she would be drawn to the meadow. There she would become aware of a bright light that would transform itself into Sojah's form. Sometimes he would mainly talk to her through her mind and she would relay his teachings to me. On other occasions, she would be taken or travel quite spontaneously to a place of interest in the Spiritual realm.

On one such journey, Marjorie found herself journeying to a very large building that felt like a Healing Temple. The walls were somehow translucent and there was a great feeling of peace and tranquility. Even though there appeared to be lots of activity going on, there was a feeling of space and ease. Sojah accompanied Marjorie here. Then she was introduced to another Spiritual being. This one appeared to Marjorie as a petite young woman with dark hair. She was excitable but also very caring and loving. She introduced herself as Dagmar, and told us that she was my Healing Guide and that her purpose was to teach about Spiritual healing and encourage me to open myself to become a channel for healing.

Dagmar deferred to Sojah, and to Marjorie's perception, Dagmar's energy was somewhat more volatile than that of Sojah. He had a calmness and depth of love to him that indicated that he was a more advanced Spiritual being. By virtue of his stature in Spirit, Sojah was allowed to teach about Spiritual matters. Dagmar's place was to practice healing and to instruct others about healing. This was a path that Dagmar had chosen for herself in Spirit, and something that she was able to communicate to Marjorie that she enjoyed very much.

In the Spiritual planes, a soul's inner nature was revealed, and souls needed to face the truth of who they were. With the higher planes, a soul could only go there when they were ready and entitled to do so. There was respect for each soul's place and much opportunity to learn, gain experience and move higher, if that is what a soul chose to do. Sojah was open to acknowledge that he was still learning and that Spiritual beings were not perfect but in a continuing process of unfoldment.

Dagmar asked me if I wanted to be a channel for her to direct healing energies through me. I agreed and initially, I practiced with Marjorie and her arthritic condition. As I proceeded, I was urged to listen for promptings from Dagmar to allow me to support her efforts. Dagmar channeled through Marjorie suggestions to help me make progress. Dagmar offered a lot of encouragement, because I needed to believe that I could be a channel and that the energies were flowing through me, so I could support the healing with my mind and through my own faith. Marjorie enjoyed the healing and found it very relaxing and soothing away the pain.

Over the months, Sojah practiced with Marjorie so that she would learn to open herself fully to his teachings and impart these without interference. She had to learn to step aside with her consciousness so that he could express his thoughts and feelings through her mind. Marjorie was a faithful pupil and Sojah was pleased with the progress that she made. For Marjorie, there was satisfaction in performing a Spiritual task, and she felt that it was something that she had been waiting all of her life to do.

We were all being prepared for the next stage, which would be for us to establish a Healing Circle where others could join in.

# Chapter 4 – The Healing Circle

It was directed by Spirit that we form a Healing Circle. Marjorie, Reg and I had been meeting together regularly for several months, becoming familiar with all the Spiritual practices that we would need.

Marjorie had been developing her skill at making contact with Sojah, and letting him channel through her. By now, she could let her consciousness step aside completely when Sojah wanted to speak, so she would have no recollection afterwards about what had been said, and would feel as if she had been resting in a very peaceful sleep while he spoke.

Sojah was able to impart much information to us about the nature of the Spiritual worlds and his own philosophy concerning life. His intention was to share his Spiritual teachings and for us to work together with him to spread these teachings and bring more Spiritual love to the Earth. He made it clear to us that his work with us was something that had been planned on a Spiritual level and it was now up to us how far we would dedicate ourselves to fulfilling the potential of what we could do together.

With Dagmar's direction, we also practiced Spiritual healing and learned how we could work co-operatively with guides and the loving force of 'God', to channel healing to help others, both directly and through absent healing, where we asked for Spirit to intercede on our behalf to administer healing to others not with us. It was interesting for us to have feedback and reflections from Dagmar as we made our efforts at healing. She helped us to develop our faith and confidence to do healing.

When it came time for us to begin our Healing Circle, Sojah suggested to us a simple format that could be applied on a regular basis as an evening ritual once a week, from which the Healing Circle could unfold. The first part of the evening would be a meditation in which we would invite Spirit to be with us and spend some time in silence to let our minds settle, let the concerns and cares of the day go, and on a personal level, to invite Spirit to support us. The second part would be to do absent healing, and to ask Spirit to send healing to people we know outside the circle that need help. This would be a simple process of going around the circle and everyone in turn speaking aloud the names of people in need with the clear intent of those people receiving healing, and then releasing that to Spirit. The third part would be to practice Spiritual Healing in pairs within the Circle. People could choose to either receive healing or channel healing to others. In channeling the healing, we would open our hearts to care for the person receiving and let the healing energies transfer to that person through our hands. The next part would involve a channeling session with Sojah, where he could speak of Spiritual matters and answer people's questions.

At the end of this session, Sojah would lead a meditation for all of us present as an inner journey for us to raise our vibrations and connect with our guides and Spirit in general more directly. The formal part of the evening would end with us holding hands and giving thanks for all the Spiritual energies that have been channelled and then releasing those energies to go where they were needed. After this, there could be some social time to enjoy the fruits of the evening and have some refreshments.

Before we invited members of the public, Marjorie, Reg and I went through the ritual of the evening without anybody else. We were happy with the ease of how the evening flowed and the beautiful energies that we felt in the house by the end of the evening.

Marjorie was anxious if she was adequate to be the hostess for the Healing Circle, but Sojah was insistent that we go ahead. We needed to place our faith and trust in Spirit, and do it.

I prepared some simple notices to put up and told people that I knew about it, and soon there was enquiries and our Healing Circle was underway.

In the first months, we attracted an assortment of people from various backgrounds and beliefs to join us. Some people were interested in the healing, others in the channeling. Not everyone could accept the channeling of Sojah, but generally, people found it to be fascinating. Sojah spoke through Marjorie with such tolerant compassion and kindness, that we noticed how much his presence affected people and helped them to feel better about themselves. The healing too, was very successful, and members of the group were able to feel many sensations and worthwhile results that could be shared with one another. Even people who did not quite believe in what we were doing, found themselves coming back week after week, because at the end of our evenings, they would feel peaceful and touched by the Spiritual influences that had been present.

We were tested sometimes, by people who felt that the evenings should be organized in a different manner, or with different emphasis, but we remained true to the structure that Sojah had laid out for us, and in time, our Healing Circle flourished.

Within a year, we had gathered together a core group of people who were very dedicated to the work of our circle. Although the members of this core group did vary over the years, now that we had a strong group that was working together, we were able to do some deeper explorations and develop further.

In his question and answer sessions, Sojah encouraged people towards learning how they could make contact with their own Spiritual guide. He explained how we all had a personal Spiritual guide who loved us and would help us as fully as they possibly could. With various members of the group, he offered advice and suggestions to help them. Sojah was also interested for people to gain direct experiences of Spiritual realities, in the manner that Marjorie could, and the meditations that he led were intended for this purpose.

Over time, many members of our group were able to achieve contact with their personal Spirit guide, and this had a transformational effect upon their lives. The Spiritual work of our Circle brought peace and contentment to our members. The presence of Spirit was strong when we met together, and this meant that when we meditated, often people could go very deep within themselves and have quite profound Spiritual experiences. We would share these, and this would encourage further Spiritual experiences to come forward. The Healing Circle was becoming a training ground for Spiritual and psychic development.

At the heart of Sojah's teachings was the path of service, where he suggested that by caring and reaching out to others, we could not only help them to be happier, but we could help ourselves to advance Spiritually as well. There was enthusiasm and inspiration in the group to go out and make a positive difference in the world. Sojah urged us to believe in ourselves that we could do this, and that Spirit would be there to guide and help us.

Close friendships developed within the group, as there was an atmosphere of support and mutual co-operation to achieve as much as we could.

People enjoyed doing the Spiritual healing and were able to practice this with people outside the circle, and these people also felt the benefits of it. There were also positive results from the absent healing we sent out, and we began to receive letters from people who felt improvement in their conditions as a result of our healing and were grateful for our help. In their daily interactions with people, members of the group noticed how much more positive and constructive they could be with others, and we shared with each other instances where this appeared to have been of help. Generally, members who were able to make contact with their Spiritual guide, were prompted by those guides to make adjustments in their lives to help them to live more to their potential and grow Spiritually. Often the kind of guidance received could be about dealing with relationships or work situations in everyday life, and making steps to improve these.

Energetically, our healing circle was like a beacon of light that shone more brightly as we continued to develop our work together.

Marjorie was delighted to have found a task in her life that was of value and helping others. She also enjoyed tremendously meeting all the many people that visited our Circle, and learn about their lives. She and her husband, Reg, would eagerly anticipate each coming meeting and dedicate themselves to looking after the people that came.

When I met with Marjorie and Reg in private, Sojah would talk with us about ways in which he wished for us to expand our work. He proposed to us that w needed to lead workshops where we could reach out to larger groups of peopl with his teaching. Sojah suggested a structure and model for such a worksho that would be an extension of what we did in the Healing Circle. We went ahea with this.

The first time we held a workshop, we had about twenty-five peopl attending along with us. Marjorie was nervous but placed her trust in Sojah. Th workshop was held in a large hall.

There was a picture of Marjorie. She was a bent frail figure, sittin uncomfortably in her wheel chair, her limbs distorted awkwardly with th arthritis. As people arrived, her eyes rose upwards and smiled i acknowledgement and welcome. She waited patiently for her time to channe Sojah. When this moment came, she allowed herself to be guided into tranc and her body slumped as normal. Then, slowly, as Sojah's consciousness entere her being to speak with everyone, her head lifted slowly and with grace. He voice rang out as clear as crystal and projected itself into the far corners of th room. People listened in silence, transfixed by the experience. For the longe session, Sojah spoke through Marjorie for well over an hour. There was a atmosphere of reverence, dignity and love that Sojah brought forward with th expression of his words. Everyone was affected. At the end, when Marjorie body returned to normal consciousness and she opened her eyes, people cam over to her and surrounded her, thanking her, sharing with her, askin questions. Marjorie did not remember anything that Sojah had said. Peopl spoke to her as if she would know. But she could feel the love of Sojah in he being. She sensed that the session had gone well and was able to cope with th people that spoke to her. Marjorie was moved to receive so much attention. I was something that had never happened to her previously. It would only b afterwards, when she was at home with Reg, that she could listen to the tap recording of what Sojah had said, and she felt pride with what she had achieved. The contrast between Marjorie's personality and that of Sojah made th channeling believable to people, that and the power and conviction with whic Sojah spoke.

Marjorie, herself, felt awe and deep respect for Sojah. When she could, sh listened intently to his recorded words, and was always impressed. There wer often surprising answers that Sojah gave that helped Marjorie with her Spiritua education. She recognized that in the way Sojah phrased thoughts and supporte people in such a considered and caring manner, that he was an independen being in his own right and not merely a sub-conscious projection of her.

The Healing Circle group continued to expand its activities. Because of th enthusiasm for Spiritual Healing, members of the group hired a room and starte ɔ offer public healing once a week. This proved very popular and provided an utlet for members of the group to further develop their skills.

Sojah offered several prophecies at various times when we conversed with im. He also did this with individuals who sought his help, and came for ndividual counselling, with Marjorie's co-operation. Mostly, his prophecies were een to come true. Examples were the establishment of the Healing group, my vriting and having my books published. He also presented a vision of a trip I vould make to Australia that turned out to be true, and made predictions about he birth of my daughter Grace, that took place many years after he first talked bout this.

One of the strongest prophecies he made was that one day in the future, as an utcome of the work with the Healing Group, there would be the establishment f a healing sanctuary, but that this would take place only after Marjorie and Reg vere no longer alive.

# Chapter 5 - The end of the Healing group and Marjorie's declin

The Healing Circle group, with Marjorie and Reg, lasted for about eight year Over this time, many members of the group made contact with their ow Spiritual guides and developed their own Spiritual and psychic gifts. Some these people tried to incorporate Spiritual practices into their professional live In the last years, more and more of the group learnt how to channel their guide so at the end of our healing evenings, rather than always having a question an answer session with Sojah, other members of the group would channel the guides instead. This was something that Sojah encouraged, an empowerment members of the group so that they would express their Spiritual gifts more full too. It represented success for Sojah with his teachings and what he had set ou to do.

However, with these other guides, came a branching out of interests and a introduction of new spheres of activity. One of these was Earth Healing, and w incorporated an Earth Healing meditation into our weekly practices. Classes an workshops were planned and carried forward. The group seemed to be goin from strength to strength.

But not all of these changes were so easy for Marjorie. While she was please that members of the group were making progress, and so much healing appeare to be taking place, on evenings where Sojah was not called to channel, she di not have a role. Because of her disability, she could not channel Spiritual Healin to others. Therefore, if Sojah was not needed, she would be sitting in the Circl all evening without feeling that she was making a contribution. Added to thi her hearing was becoming much worse, so most of what was being spoken wa not picked up by her. People in the group tried to include her, and she wa revered by many in the group for the inspiration she gave in channeling Sojah But increasingly, she felt isolated.

Marjorie watched while members of the group spoke excitedly about healin they had done or workshops and other activity that they were engaged in. Sh could not join in. Marjorie had to stay at home because she was too frail to g out. Her illness meant that she needed to take tablets continually to cope wit the level of pain she felt. The healing helped tremendously, but its effects did no last. It was not enough for her to only receive; she wanted to give as well.

In our private sessions, Dagmar and Sojah tried to encourage Marjorie to b positive and ask for their help. It was pointed out to her on many occasions ho positive thinking and imagining could make a huge difference to her conditio and how she coped. But this was not easy for her to achieve. The pain groun her down. Dagmar suggested to Marjorie that there could come a time when, a result of the healing, she would become pain free. However, I don't think th

Marjorie's faith was ever quite strong enough for that prophesy to be fulfilled.

Marjorie was more inclined to try a different strategy, and closed herself off from Spirit and people. She felt that if she did not let Spirit influence her, then things would not matter to her and she would more easily be able to endure her pain and suffering. For all her friends and loved ones, this did not seem like a very helpful approach to her life, but it was what she decided to do, and for her, it was a means for her to feel a little more control.

Sometimes the pain of her condition would become very intense and she would be afraid of it. She had panic attacks that would shake her suddenly and then the dread that these attacks would come on made her further afraid. Negative thoughts became associated with her fear, and she grew more depressed, making an inner barrier to Spirit reaching her. During these attacks, she would call out Sojah's name repeatedly in her mind, but she was only occasionally able to reach him then because her fear was too great, and she doubted that even he would be able to help.

Her physical decline reached the point where she was no longer able to hold a cup to enjoy a drink of tea at the end of our evenings. Reg had to supply a straw so she could drink her tea. She did not want people to know how frustrated she felt and how limited her physical condition had become.

Through all this, Marjorie's ability to channel remained strong and the steadfastness of Sojah's message did not waver. The contrast between Sojah's strength and loving wisdom on the one hand, and Marjorie's frailty and private pessimism on the other hand, was stark.

Sometimes, weeks went by without Marjorie channeling Sojah in the group. It is also true that Marjorie withdrew and did not put herself forward. She felt that there were members of the group that were much more interested in what their own guides had to say than anything that Sojah would teach. There was some truth in this.

It was a struggle for Marjorie. She was very loyal to our Spiritual practices, and would always try her best when people came for the group. She remained supportive of my work, and went through phases after strong Spiritual experiences, where her faith would assert itself and she would feel peace and acceptance, in spite of all her problems. The main force that pulled her down was her physical condition. She had set backs, a fall, and an operation on her hand that went wrong and left her hand disfigured and useless. The over prolonged use of steroids that in combination with the Rheumatoid arthritis had had a devastating impact on her bone structure that left her extremely fragile and in pain constantly.

The autumn of 1999 was a very unsettled time for the group. My marriage had broken up; there were others in the group facing relationship problems and job dilemmas. It was then that Marjorie announced that she had had enough. I believe that Reg would have happily continued, but Marjorie wanted to stop.

The last healing evening at Marjorie's house was just prior to the millennium. My first book, 'Healing Journeys', had just been published, so it should have been a cause for celebration, but instead there was sadness. That evening, it was Sojah who did the channeling. He spoke passionately about the new century, and all the hope, opportunities and potentials that lay ahead. It was a rousing send off to a great adventure.

The healing group continued at different venues in various forms over the following years, but it could no longer be the same. Without Marjorie and Sojah the group had lost its heart and soul. We all had to find other means of gaining our Spiritual sustenance now, and accept the ending of what had been a treasure in our lives.

For Marjorie and Reg, there was also loss. The healing group had been a blessing for them. They had met people from all over the world and been able to help and serve others. Finishing the healing group did give them space to continue their lives and retirement privately, but they did miss the lovely peaceful energy that the healing group brought with it.

The work of the Healing group touched the lives of thousands of people both directly indirectly. Many were helped to open up to their own Spiritual path and to accept the presence of Spirit more fully in their lives. It was the work of Spirit that we did in the group. Energy from the Healing and Spiritual practices we channeled in the group spread out like ripples in a lake. We must give thanks to Spirit for all the opportunities that were given to us.

# Chapter 6 – Marjorie's last years and death

Marjorie and Reg both felt that the new century brought nothing but trouble for them. Marjorie's physical condition continued to decline. She suffered tremendous amounts of pain that painkillers could not numb. Reg noticed that she would tense herself when the pain levels were up and this made her suffering worse. He would place his hands on her head, and then on her painful joints, saying prayers and asking for Spiritual help for Marjorie. Usually, this would help temporarily, and the pain would subside, making it easier for her.

Without the Healing Group, Marjorie had few visitors. She now had little in the way of social outlets and felt further isolated. In addition, because there was so little that she could do, she was often very bored. I continued to visit Marjorie and Reg most weeks, but she was less open now to her Spiritual life. There was a large part of her that had closed off from it completely. All she wanted was to die and to end her suffering.

The most devastating blow to Marjorie came when her friend Ruth died. Ruth had been the one companion besides Reg, whom Marjorie could rely on. They had daily contact. Through all the trials of their lives, Ruth and Marjorie had remained the best of friends, and Marjorie felt that she could talk about anything with Ruth, and they had so many nostalgic memories they could share. Ruth had never been part of the healing group and had a strong Catholic faith, but Marjorie still shared with her friend about this and they discussed religion quite often.

Ruth continued to pursue her acting career right up to the time of her death. For some time, she had been suffering from diabetes, and this had affected her ability to walk. But her death was very sudden and appeared to have been from a heart attack that she suffered while she was away with one of her acting jobs. Marjorie never came to terms with her loss for the rest of her life.

Some months after Ruth's death, Marjorie's brother, Charles died as well. This left Marjorie as the last remaining member of her immediate family alive. The walls of her life were closing in.

Marjorie's struggles with the Rheumatoid Arthritis had become ever more demanding as the years went on. Slowly losing her physical mobility and independence of action was demoralizing for her. When she was younger, Marjorie regarded these aspects of her as being vitally important. Yet, with time, the illness eroded increasingly her ability to act and do what she wanted. She had to ask her husband, Reg, to do for her what she wished to do herself. Although he was very devoted to her, and tried to help her as best he could, he could not give her what she most longed for. His very presence came to represent her loss of independence, something that she hated. Her mind remained clear and alert. While she was on her own for long periods, bitter thoughts festered inside her. She questioned all aspects of her life, and the way her life had turned out felt very unfair to her. The negativity of her thoughts fed from one to the other and built up a frustration that was like pressure cooker waiting to burst, with no constructive outlet. Ultimately these thoughts affected her will to live.

In that final phase of her life, Reg had to feed her, give her the tablets that she needed, carry her and transport her from one room to the next. There was hardly anything that she could manage by herself. When she looked at herself in the mirror, she saw how twisted and deformed her limbs had become. Her appearance felt to her to be ugly and she looked aged far beyond her years. For a woman, concerned with how she looked, this was very difficult to bear. When I came to visit her, she would confide that it felt humiliating what she had to suffer, and she saw no way out.

The tension between Marjorie and Reg grew daily. Marjorie's strongest thought was the desire to end her own life. As Reg had to continually support Marjorie with so many of her basic needs, she projected a lot of negativity onto him. He tried to be positive and look for the best in their situation, but this only made her angrier. They had no escape from each other, being stuck in their small house together, and Reg insisted upon being present to care for her. At times they argued and the atmosphere between them became explosive. Marjorie would sometimes vent her anger and scream at Reg to give her more tablets so that she could die. She tried to cut her wrists but did not have the strength to do it. For hours in the evenings, she would try without success to undo the bottles of her tablets. Every night, Reg would pray that Marjorie would be free from pain. It was a dilemma for him, because he hated to see her suffering so much with pain, and she would plead with him to help her die. At times she would accuse him of cruelty. But he did not feel that it was right to interfere; it was his faith that we all have our time to die. He could not play 'God', however tempting it was to do so at times.

Even though Reg had a very placid nature, there were moments when even his level of tolerance was exceeded. There were times when he when became upset and shouted, behaving right out of character because he couldn't cope with her screaming and aggressive abuse any more. Undoubtedly, they could have both benefited from more support to cope with their problems at this stage.

Occasionally, I was able to lead Marjorie on an inner Spiritual journey and then she could find peace. But it was only a brief respite. She decided that it was best for her to close the doors to Spirit and any form of hope. Marjorie felt that the best thing would be to end things as soon as possible.

How could God allow her to experience such prolonged pain and suffering?

She had tried to be good, so why should she be punished like this? How could there be a loving God behind all this? In her mind, she became determined that the experiences of Spirit must be illusions, something she made up with her subconscious mind to help her feel better.

When she consented to go on one of her inner journeys, the experience of Spirit was also like a torture. When she returned from the feeling of peace and freedom that she felt in the Spirit realm, she was sharply aware of the contrast between that and her abject physical condition. She did not want that. It was better if she could just numb the pain, somehow.

On the rare occasions when she allowed herself to connect with Sojah, he tried to sympathize with her condition and urged her to try to accept her limitations, do her best to be positive, and take one day at a time. She was always affected by his words and felt the love and care with which he approached her. But once she had returned to her normal consciousness, then after a while, the swirling of negative thoughts would return and her misery would continue.

She tried to bargain with God. Marjorie pleaded with God that because she was suffering so much, surely he could allow her the space to die? She did not have too long to wait.

One day, when Marjorie was being supported to go to the toilet, she collapsed in the corridor. Her body weight gave way and her legs would not support her. From lack of use, her muscles were too weak and her bones had become dangerously brittle through her chronic reliance on steroid tablets. The burden of having to carry and support Marjorie so much had weakened Reg too. Finally, he admitted that he needed support too. As a result of this fall, Marjorie was taken to hospital where she spent the last weeks of her life.

The grim reality of an extended stay in hospital was not easy for Marjorie to accept. She preferred to be at home. With Reg's usual optimism, he tried to imagine that Marjorie would recover and that things would work out for them. They met with social workers to consider possible plans of action for how they could manage a situation where Marjorie would be able to be at home and receive considerable outside help. But then there was another setback.

Marjorie was receiving physiotherapy to try and strengthen her muscles so that she could once more support her own weight. One day, while the physiotherapist was moving her, there was a crack in her left arm, and it broke. Her bones were too brittle and weak for the doctors to reset them. She would just have to endure the pain and discomfort that this brought her. This arm was now useless and she had to use the other one to move it about.

There were also problems with her eating. She was hardly eating any of the meals provided for her, and becoming very thin. So Reg arranged with the nurses for him to feed Marjorie, himself. This helped to give him a sense of purpose through this difficult time.

One part of Marjorie wanted everything to be over, she had had enough and needed increasing amounts of sedation. But another part of her was afraid and wished to cling on to life. She was no longer certain what would happen to her when her body died.

The positive aspect of her stay in hospital was that she enjoyed the company of the nursing staff and some of the other patients. She felt that they were very kind to her, and she loved to entertain. Marjorie carried her sincere interest in other people right through to the end of her life.

I visited Marjorie when I could, and although we tried, her mind was not settled enough to do Spiritual work. With all her inner confusion and pain, she could not cross the threshold to reach a conscious connection with Spirit. With every visit, I noticed a further deterioration in her physical condition.

On her seventieth birthday, I went to see Marjorie with my children. Although it was a happy occasion and other friends visited her too, Marjorie struggled to take in what was happening. It was an obvious effort for her to concentrate. That was the last occasion when I saw Marjorie alive.

Reg continued to attend to Marjorie's needs as he always had done. There were moments when she was bright and alert and other occasions when she appeared to be very weak. To save Marjorie pain, the nurses would pull her up by the sheets rather than trying to hold her body. From having been hostile to Reg quite often in those times leading up to this, because of her inner frustrations, in those final days, Marjorie drew a lot of comfort from holding his hand.

Once, while Marjorie was sleeping, Reg noticed that she had a wonderful smile. There was peace radiating from that smile and it made Reg feel very emotional. It felt as though somewhere inside her at that moment, she was deeply happy.

Some days before she went into hospital, Marjorie had prophesized to Reg that when it came time for her to die, then it would be as a result of breathing difficulties. That is exactly how it turned out to be.

On June 19th, some days after her birthday, Marjorie was acting quite normally during the daytime and sharing jokes with the nursing staff, but then in the evening, she complained that she could not breathe.

The doctors did not seem to be concerned. Marjorie asked Reg to remain with her, but no one from the staff indicated to Reg that he could stay, so he felt he had to go home.

At ten o'clock, the next morning, the phone went and it was the hospital. Marjorie had been asking for him, and they suggested that he come as soon as possible. Reg was most anxious, but when he did reach the ward, he found that

Marjorie was sleeping, looking very peaceful.

Over the next hours, Reg stayed with her. Marjorie mainly slept, but at intervals would open her eyes briefly, and then return to sleep. Reg reminisced about the happy experiences they had shared through their long life together.

Later in the day, the nursing sister took Reg into a room to discuss with him about Marjorie's condition. She was very gentle, but made it quite clear to him that although it was possible that Marjorie could rally, after twenty years of Rheumatoid arthritis, it was more likely that she would not. He was offered a room where he could stay, so he could be close to Marjorie at all times in case her condition deteriorated.

At nine o'clock the night staff took over. Two hours later, one of the nurses came to check Marjorie. She turned to Reg and said that it would not be long now. The lights were dimmed. By this time, Marjorie's breathing had become so shallow that it was barely perceptible. Reg placed his hand on Marjorie's arm so he could more easily sense that she was still alive.

Her life force seemed to just gently fade away. Reg was aware after she had given her final breath of air, that her life had gone.

When he left the hospital on that evening, Reg looked up at the sky. It was a very intense brilliant blue, so different from the grey weather that had been pervading during the day. Reg felt this to be a tribute to Marjorie, some kind of sign given to him.

# Chapter 7 - Encounters with Marjorie's Spiritual being

During the course of her life, Marjorie displayed an exceptional psychic gift. It is little wonder then, that during the time of her dying and after her passing, that some of those connected to her through her Spiritual work, had visions of meeting her Spiritual being.

**The time leading up to death**

Marjorie's Spiritual guide, Sojah, taught us, that as a person approaches death, especially if they have been suffering from an illness, then the Spiritual form of that person will loosen itself from the physical body in preparation for passing. In the weeks before this transition, the persons' soul could spend as much time detached from the physical body, as they would, actually in it. During the final phase of their life, people would often need to sleep a lot. As the body was resting, the soul of the person would be gaining nourishment in the Spiritual realms. Doing this would help people so that they could feel more calm and peaceful.

Many souls can be quite excited by the prospect of leaving their physical body. This might not be obvious to onlookers on the physical plane, but the act of dying means for us to return to our Spiritual home, an experience that is very joyous. It can mean meeting loved ones in Spirit, guides and generally being in a very loving environment. A soul needs to be patient with regards to this though, because we can only leave when the time is right.

I have heard numerous accounts of people, who, when dying, talked of meeting loved one that were already on the other side. One client of mine, a woman that I will call Sandra, gave an account relating to her dying mother. One day, her mother was in a state of semi-consciousness when she appeared to be having a conversation with her dead husband, as if he was there. Sandra's mother was oblivious to Sandra's presence. The conversation continued in a normal fashion. It was as though her mother's consciousness was in another realm, but still sufficiently attached to her physical body for her to be able to speak and be heard.

In the case of Marjorie during her last weeks, we have the instance of the very peaceful smile that Reg witnessed while she was sleeping. Other indications that she might have been slipping away during this period include the fact that she was sleeping a lot, and also that her attitude towards Reg softened considerably and became much more loving again.

One of my clients, Alice, lived very close to Marjorie and Reg. Although she was in her nineties, Alice had a clear mind and openness to Spirit. She had only met Marjorie on a few occasions, but one of these was to experience Marjorie channeling her guide, Sojah. This had impressed Alice greatly. In addition, Alice had read my book, 'Healing Journeys', and through my regular contact with her to do Spiritual Healing, she felt a strong sympathy and devotion to Marjorie.

As part of my work with Alice, she practiced meditation to enable her to strengthen her conscious connection with her own Spiritual guide and to help her to find peace. Over the months that we had been working together, I had prepared tapes for her with suggestions and guided inner journeys to help her achieve this. She would listen to these tapes daily, and sometimes gain great benefit from them.

Throughout her life, Alice had shown sensitivity to Spirit, although she had not always lived in circumstances where she could nurture this. On a number of occasions, she had become aware of the Spiritual presence of relatives who had passed over and she had been able to have conversations with these beings.

On one afternoon, shortly after Marjorie's admission to hospital, Alice was playing one of my tapes, when she found herself going into a deeper meditation than usual. Suddenly, she was aware of the presence of Marjorie talking to her. She recognized clearly that it was Marjorie in her Spiritual form. At first, Alice was quite startled and questioned Marjorie whether she had already left the physical plane. Marjorie replied that she had not, but she insisted that it would not be long before she did pass over.

Marjorie then became very agitated. She expressed that she was very anxious and worried about her husband, Reg, and how he would cope after she had gone. Marjorie asked Alice to undertake that she would help to look after him. Alice promised to do what she could. With this, Marjorie appeared to be quite comforted. Alice then felt Marjorie's energy fade until, very soon, she was no longer aware of her presence.

It is interesting to note that at the time, Reg and Alice were barely acquainted with each other. However, in the months following Marjorie's death, they struck a friendship and met regularly. It was clear that Reg derived a great deal of support from this, and was something that nourished both of them.

**The transition following death**

The process of going through death is unique to every individual, but has elements that are common for everybody. Marjorie's Spiritual guide, Sojah, taught us that we all have a silver cord, an energy line that links our physical body with our greater Spiritual self. During our lives, we can leave our physical bodies, psychically, and often we will do this to go on journeys while we sleep, for instance, but we remain connected to our physical self through this cord. The cord will stretch with us as we travel. When we near Death, this silver cord weakens, and at the moment of Death, will be severed completely. Then our consciousness will leave the physical body permanently without the possibility of return, and the substances comprising the physical body will no longer have that Spiritual force associated with the human soul to unite them. There will be an imprint of that human soul that remains with the substances of the physical body. This imprint will nourish the spirit of the Earth as those elements of the body return to their constituents.

Where we go after our physical body dies is according to our will. Those with strong faith will inexorably be drawn upwards to the light, to a Spiritual realm that is almost overwhelming with its love and peace. It will be a real feeling of coming home for the soul. In this place, there will be joyful meetings with other souls and further processes that need to be undertaken.

Others could have the wish not to leave the place where they have been. They may have emotional ties to people or the place itself, and want to stay where it feels familiar. There will be a strong draw for souls to move on and rise upwards towards the light of Spirit, but some might need to process what has happened to them before they are ready to make that transition. Others may not be open and could become Earthbound Spirits. Some could even be afraid of facing 'God' out of fear concerning whatever punishment they feel could be due to them because of their actions while in the physical body. Refusing to join their greater self in the Spiritual realm can be lonely and isolating. Eventually, these souls will have enough and be desperate to move on. By reaching out to be open for help, these souls will be shown how they could rise up to their Spiritual home, but the choice to do so will be left to them.

It is also possible that souls can become lost in some in between realm. Because of their limiting thoughts and beliefs, these souls could remain in some quite dark place imprisoned by their own inner expectations. They might have decided through religious conviction or their own will about how the nature of reality should be for them, and be unwilling to accept anything different. These souls can remain stuck then as a result of their own rigid ideas rather than being open for the truth to express itself to them. It will only be when, perhaps out of boredom and frustration that these souls become open to change and the possibilities of other realities that they can move on.

During the years that Marjorie channelled to us, she was sometimes able to allow a range of Spirits to speak through her of their story of what happened to them when they died. These stories could be fascinating and invariably the journey that these souls undertook following death reflected closely the reality they had built up in their minds while in the physical body. The process of uniting with the Spiritual realm, was associated with those souls learning how they could free themselves of limiting beliefs they had gathered while on Earth and perceiving a greater truth that was there waiting to be revealed to them.

One of the beings that Marjorie channeled was someone I will call Walter. He was an atheist and he told how he was very firmly of the opinion that physical death would mark the end of his existence. When his body died, he found himself in a dark place but he was still conscious. It took Walter some time to accept this, and only after a long time did he then open to the possibility that other beings could also exist. As soon as he allowed this thought, Walter became aware of a bright light above him, that became ever brighter as he welcomed it, and then he merged into the love and light of Spirit and felt a lot better. Walter realized that his life had been quite barren because he had not permitted the wonders of Spiritual thoughts to be part of his life. There were small miracles in his everyday life for which he could have been thankful and the awareness of this would have enriched his life, but he remained closed to them.

Spirit permeates all life. When we open our minds to this, we will perceive the true beauty of all existence, whether this is a flower, someone's smile or the rain falling. This will bring a feeling of joy into our hearts. We will feel how we are connected to that which is around us, and that will add meaning to our lives. For someone with no Spiritual belief, life is perceived on material terms only, and there will not be the same feeling of connection or joy. Atheists will be limited in what they can perceive of the true beauty of life because their minds are closed to it.

All life has its own Spiritual path and journey. As human beings, we also have our own Spiritual path, which we have chosen on the level of our soul. With each waking day, there are Spiritual influences and guidance coming to us so that our encounters with people and nature can have meaning to help us to be true to our Spiritual path if we are awake to it.

Another being that Marjorie channeled was a woman that I will call Julia. She had a more traditional Christian view of life. She did believe in God but had a more narrow view about what 'heaven' would be like when she died. Julia had a concept of Jesus and the angels and expected that she would only meet other Christians in 'heaven' when she passed over. Her thoughts of this were quite strong, and when she did die, she did indeed meet Jesus and came into a world that reflected her Christian beliefs. However, it was only when she became receptive to the idea that there were others in Spirit besides those that shared the Christian beliefs that she had had on Earth, that the brilliance and fullness of love of the Spiritual realm became manifested to her. After this change, Julia met Jesus in Spirit once more. He was teaching to a group of interested souls. The experience of meeting Jesus now, was so much more profound. Julia realized how dull life had appeared to her, due to the limitations of her own beliefs.

It appears that many souls need a process to adjust to the Spiritual realm when their physical bodies die. Some progress quickly into the light and are ready to meet other souls, review their path and continue on their journey. Our beliefs make a huge contribution to our perceptions, and so if when at the point of our death, our perceptions are not in accordance with the greater reality known to our Spiritual self, then we will need guidance to learn so that the various aspects of our being can integrate. Once integration has occurred, our awareness will be opened to a much greater degree.

There are indications from when Marjorie died, about the adjustment process that was needed for her before she could fully rise up to her Spiritual self, as the following account will indicate.

**Marjorie's transition**

When Marjorie was close to dying, although she appeared to be confused, no longer prepared to believe in Spirit, feeling afraid and uncertain as to what would await her when she died, I sense that at a deeper level, she was quite knowledgeable and ready for what would happen to her. Whatever she professed on the surface of her consciousness, I know that her inner faith was clear and unshakeable.

Several people reported meetings with Marjorie's soul in the weeks following her death. These do correlate to give impressions of how Marjorie's soul was progressing. I feel that it is quite normal for souls to need a period of time to fully release all vestiges of their attachments to the physical plane. When it takes a whole lifetime to build these up, we need a process of slow withdrawal to let them go.

From those experiences that I know about, my wife, Eleyna, was the first person to perceive Marjorie's being after her death. Eleyna had been a member of the Healing group that Marjorie, Reg and I founded. In this group, she had developed her psychic gifts and the Spiritual capacity to connect with her own guide. Eleyna particularly enjoyed channeling Spiritual healing. When she did this, she discovered, as she tuned into people, that she would sometimes feel their pain or discomfort in her own body. Invariably, the places where she felt this in her self, would correspond to the places in the other person's body that needed healing.

Eleyna had the utmost respect for Marjorie. She valued Marjorie's Spiritual integrity and her kindness. When Marjorie died, Eleyna was greatly affected by this. With her mind, she consciously asked that if Marjorie was there, that she could make herself known and communicate to her.

At that time, Eleyna was in good health and had no problems that caused her any physical discomfort. However, the next morning, when Eleyna got up and put her feet on the ground, she felt a painful ache come up through the balls of her feet, making it difficult for her to walk. As she tried to come down the stairs, she struggled. It was as if every bone and every joint in her body was racked with pain. Then it occurred to her that Marjorie was with her. Eleyna had taken on the symptoms of physical pain that Marjorie had suffered with her arthritis condition.

Inwardly, Eleyna perceived Marjorie to be fit and well. She was no longer deformed and seemed in her energy about twenty or thirty years younger than at the time of her death. It felt to Eleyna that Marjorie was still in the process of integrating herself with the Spiritual dimension of reality. She asked Marjorie to tell her what it was like in Spirit and Marjorie replied that she wasn't fully there yet.

Eleyna was curious to know why Marjorie chose to contact her, and Marjorie replied that Eleyna was the only one to have asked. I haven't been able to verify this, but that is the answer that Marjorie gave.

As Eleyna prepared to go to her work, the feelings of aches and pain subsided. However, the next morning, Eleyna experienced the same painful symptoms again, to a lesser extent. After that, she felt that Marjorie was gone.

Some days later, Marjorie's funeral was held at the local crematorium. It was a very touching and poignant occasion. It feels natural that Marjorie's Spirit being would be drawn close by all the tributes that were being paid to her.

Jill was one of those who attended. She had been a loyal member of the healing group since a time near to its conception in the early 1990's. Whilst Jill was very saddened by Marjorie's death, she recognized that for Marjorie, her death must have come as a blessed relief. Several times in the months before her death, Jill had had conversations with Marjorie. During these interchanges Marjorie had repeatedly expressed her wish to die and end the suffering that she endured. Although Jill valued Marjorie's qualities very much, it pained Jill to witness her friend in such distress.

Throughout the funeral ceremony, Jill sat in the middle of the gathering of people who had come to honour Marjorie and offer their respects to her. From the outset, Jill had the distinct feeling that Marjorie's being was present. To her perception, she felt that Marjorie was dancing around the room, and particularly, up and down the central aisle. Marjorie appeared much younger than Jill had ever known her. She looked about thirty years old with quite long, curly, black hair. Jill perceived that Marjorie was wearing a summer dress and seemed to be really happy. It was as though she was expressing a sense of liberation and gladness to be released from that awful body. Watching her gave Jill a feeling of elation.

Jill was not the only one to perceive Marjorie's presence during the funeral. Another member of the Healing group, Lynda, also became aware of Marjorie's being at one stage of the funeral service. However, Lynda was seated right at the back of the room where the ceremony was held. Her vision of Marjorie came to her quite independently to that of Jill, but their accounts tally remarkably. Lynda was someone with an acute psychic sensitivity, so it was not surprising that she was able to perceive Marjorie's Spirit form during this occasion.

The climax of the funeral service was marked by a tape playing one of Marjorie's favourite pieces of music, the theme from 'Olathe'. At this point, Lynda observed Marjorie with her psychic sense to be at the front of the aisle where Reg and his family were seated. She was wearing a pure, white dress, very flowing, with a full skirt. Her hair was long, thick and over her shoulders, much different from the short, cropped, thinning hair that Lynda had experienced from Marjorie's later years. Her face was young and alive looking, about the same age that Jill had intuited. There was a sparkle of joy and fun in her eyes.

As the music continued, Marjorie danced very energetically down the aisle towards the back. She was kicking her legs very high to the music. There was a sense of absolute euphoria in her manner.

In her mind, Lynda heard the words: 'Look at me. I can do this now!' It was as though Marjorie was rejoicing in her newly found freedom.

When Marjorie reached the row where I was seated with my family, Lynda observed that she stopped and looked at me. Very gently and affectionately, she reached out and touched me in the middle of my back. Then, with a little tap, she whirled away to the music once more. Lynda noticed some further details of her clothes, in that she appeared to be wearing red shoes and a shawl around her shoulders. After a few additional, lively, joyful exaggerated movements, she vanished from Lynda's perception.

For my own part, I did not have any awareness of Marjorie's presence during the service. However, I do remember during the music that there were moments where I felt quite emotional, and I found myself missing Marjorie and all that she had been in my life.

Following the funeral, Reg and Alice began to attend our Friday evening Healing evenings. For about a month after this, during these meetings, there were people that felt Marjorie's presence to be very close while we were meditating together. This brought with it, quite a strong feeling of love and was of some comfort to Reg in particular. On one occasion, Jill sensed Marjorie's voice offering her a message for Reg, urging him not to be sad; it had been a time for her to be free of that body and she was very happy now.

Meanwhile, Alice also had a further vision of Marjorie while at home. One day when she had returned from a shopping trip, Alice felt that she had to sit down, and so she sank into her favourite chair and relaxed. She quickly went into a very deep state and heard Marjorie's voice in her mind. From this, she knew immediately that Marjorie's Spiritual being wanted to speak with her.

Exchanging greetings, Alice sensed Marjorie's voice to be pleasant and clear.

The most interesting topic in this conversation occurred when Alice asked Marjorie what she was doing to occupy herself. Marjorie then replied that her main activity was working in the Spiritual nursery attending to the babies.

Sojah had taught us that the souls of unborn children and young children that died would be looked after and loved in Spirit by a dedicated team of Spiritual beings. These young Spirit children would be able to play, explore, learn and grow. The Spirit nursery existed as a compensation for these souls for experiences that they had missed out on in the physical body and a chance for them to express what had only been there in potential for them on the physical plane. It was a very happy and beautiful place, where souls who had been mothers could also unite with their young children in Spirit if they had been separated in emotional or tragic circumstances on the physical plane.

I speculate whether Marjorie may have met up with the souls of her own unborn children in this nursery, something that would have surely been very joyful for her, but Marjorie did not make this explicit in her communication with Alice.

On the following Friday at the healing evening, Alice again had contact with Marjorie. She told Alice during the meditation, that she would soon be moving to a higher plane, to a place of learning where she needed to go, but she was pleased with the amount of support being offered to Reg. This contact was like a farewell, and Marjorie's presence was not noticed at the healing evenings after that.

It was around this time that Reg had his own vision of Marjorie, an inner perception that moved him profoundly. In the period following Marjorie's death, Reg had been going though a vast range of emotional experience. He had been desperate for Marjorie to come to him in her Spirit form and give him some evidence of her survival. It is possible that because he wanted it so much with his will, that this could have blocked the channels to communication, but also it could have been a test for Reg. When other people were reporting meetings with Marjorie's Spiritual being, it was very frustrating for him that until now, he had not.

Reg's life had been very closely intertwined with that of Marjorie, so it was a poignant question he had to ask himself about what his life could be about now that she was gone. He needed to ask himself whether or not he wanted to live, and if so, to find a meaning and purpose to go on. This was a very personal search for Reg and a very difficult one at times. He was not one to reach out for support so easily in the manner that Marjorie had done, but he preferred to work out his inner dilemmas privately, without bothering others.

Reg has a strong soul though, with an enduring faith, and this was a challenge he could meet. It was only when he had become determined that he would go on, and he was starting to seek out activities for his own fulfillment, that Marjorie appeared to him. But first, there was another test.

One evening, Reg awoke to find that there was a fire that had started outside his flat. The blaze of this fire caused extensive damage and resulted in Reg needing to be given shelter in a nearby hotel while repairs were undertaken. Many people would not have coped with an ordeal such as this, especially following so soon after Marjorie's death, but Reg refused to be broken.

One evening, while in this hotel, Reg was sorting out clothes in his room, when suddenly, he felt a cold sensation at the back of his neck that made him shudder. Reg wondered if this could be his body reacting to the stress of his situation so he tried to ignore it. Then, as he continued with his chores, the feeling dissipated, but he felt heaviness in his mind and the compelling urge to sleep.

Closing his eyes, Reg saw Marjorie walking slowly towards him with her arms outstretched. She was carrying a box. In her physical life, during the months before she died, she was so crippled that she could hardly even lift a fork or spoon. Having this box in her arms was remarkable and it seemed deliberate on her part that she wanted to show him this.

In appearance, Marjorie looked well and was smiling. She was wearing a striped top and a pair of slacks. There was a strong atmosphere of love. She asked Reg if he would like to see the dwelling place in Spirit where she lived. Marjorie called it her flat.

Reg saw Marjorie sitting at a large round table that seemed transparent like glass. He noticed two cupboards, but the scene was without colour, as if only some aspects of this environment could be communicated to Reg. As Reg tried to observe more details, it all faded, and he woke up.

The fact that his vision did not include colour made the whole experience more believable for Reg. Previously, all his visions had been in colour and it is what he would have expected with this too.

Overall, Reg was convinced that this revelation was a genuine contact with Marjorie. It helped his faith and was an affirmation for him to continue with his life. He had needed her love, and in this vision, felt that had had been given it.

With regards to my own experiences, in those fragile months before and after Marjorie's death, I did not personally feel that I had any direct contact with her Spiritual being. However, I did not seek for it either. Somewhere inside, I knew that my time to commune with her Spirit being would be later, when I came to write this book, and so it turned out to be.

# Chapter 8 - Channeling Marjorie in Spirit

One day when I was channeling healing to Alice, I suddenly felt the energetic presence of Marjorie with me. Thoughts of her filled me and I experienced euphoric emotions connected with the relationship that I had shared with her. Before this, I had not been thinking of Marjorie. It just came to me unexpectedly. Some months had passed since Marjorie's death, and it was as if she was letting me know that she was there and that she was now available for me. I felt it like a beginning and I was quite excited that soon I might be able to relate to her Spiritual being more fully.

While Marjorie had been alive, her guide, Sojah, had told me on more than one occasion, that one of the best ways for me to develop my channeling abilities, was through a form of automatic writing, where I would go into a semi-meditative state and allow the thoughts of Spirit to come to me, and then spontaneously write them down. Intuitively, I felt that this would be the most effective means for me to channel Marjorie's spirit. I needed a clear and quiet space where I could go within myself and be with Marjorie on my own.

To manifest this situation, I had to wait until after the first anniversary of her death. If I was to attempt to do this work in the midst of my busy everyday life, I felt that I would be likely to compromise the clarity of what I would be channeling. I needed to be in a place where I was very relaxed and where there were few other demands or responsibilities distracting me.

During that summer, there were five days during which I visited NewBold House, a Spiritual retreat centre in Scotland, for a short break, while my wife was working. It was an ideal opportunity. I felt very much at ease with myself over these days, and decided that I would try to contact Marjorie in the meditation sanctuary there. It was an environment where I felt very sensitive, and I was confident of success.

While at NewBold House, I had one session in the sanctuary every day, four sessions in all. Each one lasted about an hour. They blended very easily into my life there and I felt a profound atmosphere of peace in the sanctuary while I continued my investigations. I was very pleased with the outcome and have included transcripts of these sessions over this chapter and the next.

Although I dedicated myself to focus upon channeling Marjorie, those in Spirit appeared to have other ideas. In sessions three and four, I found myself going to a deeper level of meditation where I was taken to meet with Marjorie's Spiritual guide, Sojah. This was the first time that I had spoken directly with Sojah through my mind, and I felt quite nervous about it when it happened, but I did my best to be faithful to what he wanted to impart. The transcripts of these two sessions are in the next chapter. Here follows the first two transcripts:

**Session 1**

In my meditation, I quietly repeated Marjorie's name. Then, more and more, I became aware of a light presence on the upper right side of my mind.

*I want to reach you, Paul,* a voice said, and it seemed to be leading me slowly upwards.

*Paul, you need to be very quiet for this. Really, just put your other thoughts to one side.* There was a gentle but firm urgency in the tone of the voice that I heard. I recognized its energy as that of my own personal guide, Sebastian, talking to me. But the first voice had been that of someone else. I hoped that it could be Marjorie.

*Come with me,* the voice beckoned. *I want to show you the beauty of the place where I am now living. I am free now. Look how well I can move. In this realm, Paul, there are no limits to my movements. It is a marvelous feeling.*

When I sensed Marjorie's energy, it was much fuller, and more complete in her soul being than when I had known her in her physical body. She had a brilliant light and vibrancy about her. There was much that she wanted to say to me.

*I have to constrict myself a lot so that you will be aware of me. But I have been training for this. Sojah has been helping me. I want you to meet him, more as he truly is, for he is a magnificent being. I had to learn a lot to be able to adjust to him, so that I could be more fully in his presence.*

*You see, when I came over, I was very confused. I was, of course, aware of all the Spiritual light and other Spiritual beings when my body died as Marjorie. I even saw Sojah. But I did not want to believe that they were there. I wanted to believe that there was nothingness and emptiness, because that is what I had tried to convince myself was the nature of reality. I had decided that there would be no life after death, because with my will, I wanted so much to die, and I couldn't hold that position when I was open to the belief that Sojah would be there waiting for me. He might have told me that I would have to live longer, and I didn't want that. I had had enough.*

*In fact, a window of opportunity, where I could die, was opened for me because I wanted it so much, and I accepted it when it came. I realize now that if I had remained open with my faith, I might have lived longer and did some more Spiritual work. My body could have remained in better condition for longer too. Through the attitude of my mind, I stopped Spiritual help from reaching me, and my thoughts about my life became like a prison, and I desperately wanted to get out. By closing the doors on my faith, I also had become afraid of death, because I didn't have anything to assure me of what it would be like.*

*It took me a while to accept Sojah and the other Spiritual life, because it made all my efforts at trying to suppress their existence into a lie. I could jump and dance and skip about, of course, but there was more going on for me than that.*

*Poor Reg was left there on his own. And I felt devastated for him. I had been so cruel to him, you see, criticizing him, tormenting him, and being angry with him, when he was only trying to help me. He didn't deserve all those things, but it was only because I didn't want help that he repulsed me and I felt the need to reject him. I wanted an end to suffering and I didn't want to feel those painful limitations anymore. I had to direct my frustrations somewhere, and sadly, it was poor Reg, who was the one to get it.*

*I tried to contact Reg on more than one occasion, but it was difficult for me to get through. And I couldn't stay all that long either. After a while, I had to go to this most beautiful healing hall, where I could rest and sort myself out.*

*Meeting Sojah, as he really is, was the most amazing experience, Paul. He is so much more vast and wise as a presence than I had ever been able to imagine in physical form. He had so much love to offer me, and although I was deeply disappointed at my own efforts in that life, he comforted me, and assured me, that essentially, I had done what I set out to do. By channeling him, and by allowing the Spiritual truths that he wanted to teach, to be spread outwards, I fulfilled the main purpose that I had come to do.*

*You see, in some of my past lives, I had refused to allow my psychic gifts to be developed, because I was afraid of them, and there were other times where I had used these gifts wrongly. This time, it was important for me to accept them, and to accept Sojah, someone greater than myself, and to be humble in his presence. And I know now that our work has touched a great many people, and it will continue to do so.*

*Sojah has taken me to some of the higher planes, as far as I can go, to show me more about what his existence is like. I can hardly begin to describe it to you. It is a tremendous field of creativity, love and manifested thought processes. I still feel in awe of him, and he has promised me that he is going to continue to watch over me and assist me as much as he is able, even though our partnership from my life, as Marjorie, is over.*

*Although I have journeyed to experience some important moments with the children here in Spirit – and I had to meet my own, the ones I couldn't carry to be born – I have been more drawn to study and gain knowledge about the different planes of existence. We have many fine teachers here, and the true nature of reality is so much more intricate than I ever imagined while on Earth.*

*As Marjorie, I was very impressed by Sojah's knowledge, and I had a great, unfulfilled thirst to learn more about the possibilities of Spirit life, and that is what I mainly do here. I am considering that for my next life on Earth, I may plan to be a scholar, because for so many lives, my desire to be educated, and to gain knowledge, has not been met. So, I have very much enjoyed having the mental faculties of my mind stimulated, placing thoughts within me that are like potentials that could be consolidated through further physical experience.*

*When I was Marjorie, I did not wish for any further physical experience, but now I see the sense in it. It is difficult to explain, but although I can learn here in Spirit and learn much that is very valuable, if I can realize even some small threads of that learning while in physical incarnation, it will make the development of my soul, so much stronger.*

*It is like a plant gaining roots in your world. Physical life can give roots to knowledge and other experiences, and thereby help the love of the soul to grow in ways that otherwise would be very difficult unless that soul was advanced enough.*

*But there is much more for me to learn. I am studying now because I want education and academic learning to be an important component of my development for the future. My soul needs it so that it will be more whole and complete.*

*There are other teachers, not as high as Sojah, who help me to advance my studies.*

At this point, I felt that I needed to stop. I had been in communion with Marjorie for about an hour, and I could sense that my concentration was starting to waver. Coming out of the meditation, I felt very calm and tranquil, an inner feeling of gratitude for what had just passed.

**Session 2**

As I sat down once more in the meditation sanctuary at NewBold House, there were thoughts welling up inside me about Marjorie. I felt that she was very close and eager to continue what she had started the previous day. In my mind, it was as though the agenda of the main topics that she would be sharing with me today were already forming themselves. Marjorie wanted to discuss with me further about her life in Spirit, about meeting her best friend, Ruth, and about the nature of the various planes where she had travelled and learnt.

When I closed my eyes, I felt Marjorie's presence again on the upper right part of my mind. Her presence was light, and thoughts from her were clear. She started talking to me about Ruth.

Earlier in the book, I mentioned how Marjorie and Ruth were like sisters. Ruth was a quite famous actress who had appeared in many TV productions including 'Coronation Street'. They had many deep discussions about the meaning of life, and when Ruth died about two years before her own death, Marjorie found this very hard. This is what she conveyed to me:

*I missed Ruth terribly when she died, and it was like a large part of me died with her. I gave up and didn't see the point of trying any longer. Although I desired very much to contact her in Spirit, there was another part of me that blocked her because I didn't want to believe anymore.*

*I have met Ruth now, and I am so glad I did. She told me that she tried to reach me, because she felt the pull from me that I so much wanted her, but she couldn't approach me because I also had a strong barrier there that did not want to listen. You see, I wanted her to be there and yet I did not want her to be there at the same time. By her not being there, it falsely proved to me that there was no such thing as Spiritual life, because if there were, she would have been sure to contact me.*

*Ruth has been studying the scriptures. She was also very confused at the time of her passing. Although she had a very strong religious desire, she was very uncertain about what was true, and she didn't want to be in a position where she would have to suffer in a dark place when she came here. Ruth has studied with some of the angelic beings, and even been present at some of the gatherings with the Master, Jesus. I went with her once, and it was a fantastic experience. There has been so much for me to learn about these matters too.*

*A lot of doctrines concerning Christianity have been misinterpreted mistakenly. Essentially, Jesus was a simple man. He wanted to heal, and demonstrate through his being, the power of Spiritual love. He lived as an example to which other people can aspire. He was able to release a lot of Spiritual energy upon the Earth, especially when he died. And that energy is still being released. When people on Earth welcome the Spiritual energy of Jesus into their hearts, it does help to bring more of that Spiritual love onto your world. But it not only through Jesus that Spiritual love can be channeled into physical life on Earth. And this is where some people have misinterpreted Jesus' intentions.*

*Ruth is very happy in her life here. Although we visit each other often, we are on a slightly different track of learning to each other now. In Spirit, I don't feel that I need her nearly to the same extent that I thought I did while I was Marjorie. We have both moved on, and we are content with the ways where we are going.*

*As I have mentioned, the main thrust of my own learning, has been in studying the various planes of existence. Sojah mentioned about the planes many times in his teachings, and he has granted me the privilege of journeying to some of the higher planes, that on my own, I would not be able to reach. Since leaving my body as Marjorie, I have travelled to many Spiritual places that have quite fascinated me.*

*It is hard for me to know how to impart all this to you. As you go higher in the planes, the nature of reality is much more pure energy patterns, thought creations and strata of love. There has been so much for me to absorb into my little being. I have met many outstanding teachers trying to pass on knowledge. Because I felt so restricted in my physical body as Marjorie, I had gathered to myself a tremendously strong unexpressed urge to travel and explore. Sojah has helped give me ideas and direction as to how I can do that.*

*I have been to see the members of my family, the ones that I knew as family when I was Marjorie. It was very joyful to see them all, but also hard, particularly with my father. He was very sorry that he hadn't shown me more love and kindness during our life together. But I could forgive him as I realized his own upbringing had been extraordinarily harsh, and it was very challenging for him to give love when he didn't feel that he had been given much love himself. But I think it affected me, and I sometimes brooded on it, and never said much about it to anyone except maybe Ruth. He is one soul that I am probably going to have to meet again, for us to become more loving to each other.*

*You can perceive things much clearer here. Secrets in relationships aren't hidden anymore. But we still need to decide things and work things out. Unless we are open to it, we may not be able to see all the perspectives in a situation. That is where we need wiser teachers that can help us to understand more fully the patterns of learning we are undergoing as souls and what may be most needed to move this forward for all concerned.*

*Apart from my sister, Joan, though, I don't have a lot to do with those other souls that were my family then. There are other souls with whom I am more closely bonded. Joan and I have a lot of links and we have been siblings many times. She has continued to study the arts and creative self-expression since she came here. It is amazing the energy structure that can be manifested through creative expression. There are, in a way that you might struggle to understand, concerts and performances here in Spirit. This gives Spiritual beings the opportunity to marvel and appreciate the possibilities of what can be manifested. It is a form of service in which Joan's soul excels.*

*I tried to show Reg a vision of where I lived and the house that I had created for myself. But it was only on the plane that is usually called the Summerland, and was only an intermediate place for me to be until I was ready to go higher. Now I have a very different place of my own. It has beautiful colours and thought designs to make it attractive for other souls to visit. Again, with me having been so restricted physically when I lived as Marjorie, it has been very important for me to feel able to generate the energy of a wholesome home, where I can rest and gather my energies towards purposeful activity. I have gained a great deal of satisfaction doing this.*

*I still take an interest in you, Paul, and your work, as well as Reg. There is a window from my dwelling place through which I am allowed to observe to some degree, the range of your activities. But I cannot interfere, and it is rare that I am allowed to approach closely, because I have moved on with my journey, and I have not acquired the responsibility of guiding.*

*It is through your guides, Paul, and Sojah, that I am able to reach you today, in this session. This is something that was arranged and planned and so it is fulfilling a soul contract that we had. It was something that we both agreed, as souls, to make this contact after my passing, as an attempt to spread further, knowledge of the Spiritual worlds and how they function. Thank you, Paul, for listening. I feel I need to go now.*

# Chapter 9 - A meeting with Sojah

On the third occasion that I went to the NewBold House meditation anctuary, to attempt to channel Marjorie, again, I closed my eyes, and allowed nyself to drift into that familiar meditative passively aware state. Within the NewBold sanctuary, the atmosphere of the room was very silent and peaceful. It elt natural in this environment to let myself drift inwards, and here, I could ccomplish a state of inner stillness easily.

When I entered into these meditations, I had to let the process unfold of its wn accord. This time had elements of the unknown to me. I did not have a ense of what would happen like the previous meditation. I felt then that I had omehow completed my contact with Marjorie and did not know what would happen next. Because of my intentions, I did not know quite how to proceed xcept to seek for Marjorie's Spirit's presence again.

I started as usual by inwardly repeating Marjorie's name, as if by invoking her name, I would draw her being to me. Soon there was a response, and I heard a voice calling for me to come, and I knew it was Marjorie.

Marjorie's presence in Spirit felt very light and free, so different from how I knew her in physical form. Yet, I could still recognize her qualities and being as Marjorie'. Today, I sensed that she was dancing and singing to me, and in my awareness, I felt myself lifted higher and higher, as if her dancing movements were actually lifting me upwards.

Soon, I sensed myself to enter a realm that was very light, and it was like a waiting area, open, and yet strangely enclosed and private, in a completely non-hreatening way. Marjorie's movements had slowed now, but I could feel her xcitement. I felt nervous, myself.

Instinctively I felt drawn to tune into Sojah, to make that connection. I found myself calling his name, repeating it deep inside, just as I had done with Marjorie. There was something compelling about doing this. I had to go on. Then suddenly, I was aware of a very light presence. It was as though I had to shield my inner eyes to adjust to the brilliance.

Sojah spoke to me, and his words etched deep into my mind.

*Welcome Paul. I have been waiting for this moment to speak with you. It has been my wish to teach and spread knowledge of the Spiritual realms to the people of your world. You and Marjorie were the two souls that were chosen to help me, and I must not forget the assistance of Reg. It is good that you agreed to do this because it helps all of us in our progress as souls. Marjorie's work as a physical agent for channeling my thoughts is over. She was largely successful in her task.*

*Now we are all engaged in further Spiritual work that was also planned and needs to be fulfilled. Today, I am asking if you can be the channel, Paul. I know that you are nervous about this, but I will protect you. In reaching out to me and calling my name, you have done your part. We both know that you are not gifted in the same capacity for psychic channeling as Marjorie. And it is not in your plan to do this publicly in the same manner as Marjorie did. But if you are willing, I will try to convey my thoughts to you to write.*

I felt myself agree to this, and then he continued.

*Paul, I am trying to speak with you, trying to adjust to your frequency. It is a little difficult, because I have never done this before with you. You are used to tuning with your own guides, and I am a little different. I have come down quite a long way to reach you, and with Marjorie's help, we have tried to assist you to raise your frequency to receive me. Gradually, I feel that we are getting there.*

*I send you greetings and I am so glad that you are doing this work and seeking contact with Marjorie and myself. Marjorie has been waiting to do this since the time that she passed over, and I have been trying to support her to be patient with you. In your world, things sometimes take a little longer and are a little more complicated than we are able to appreciate on our side. Still, you are now with us and I will try and pass on some knowledge and thoughts that I hope will be helpful to you and your readers.*

*My name is Sojah, and although I have progressed a little further since the time of Marjorie's passing, due to my work with her, I still reside mainly in the seventh plane of existence, where I am continuing my work of channeling love, energy and help to those souls that have passed over and lost their way, and are refusing to open themselves to anything except their own thoughts and self-pity.*

*I wanted to share with you a little bit about Marjorie and how proud I have been of her. The life challenges she chose were not easy ones. The greatest challenge was for her to accept me and let herself be used as a channel for my teachings to be given. This was a big test, given the pain and suffering that she had to endure. To let me in, she had to open her heart and believe. And she did this. Even though, in her later years, she tried to shut me out, and yearned for an end of all her pain, deep in her heart she continued to know that I was there, and she did the work that was required of her. The publication of your first book gave her great joy, as did the classes and workshops that you held together.*

*She knows now that on a soul level, her lifetime as Marjorie was largely successful, and she has now recognized the merit of her achievement and received her reward in the advancement of her soul to a higher level. This is not something that she expected, and she felt much joy when the truth of her endeavours was explained to her.*

*You see, much of Marjorie's lesson was about opening her heart. For her to let me be there with her and channel, there was a great deal of Spiritual love that she needed to embrace. Many people would shy away from that and decide that it was too much or them. Marjorie did not have a lot of confidence in herself, but what she did in onsciously working with me, was to offer a service to others. The main reason that he contacted me was to help you and because she thought that it might help others. he was humble and therefore able to accomplish her task.*

*Her illness was meant to be a means of restricting the scope of her activities so hat she would value more the opportunity of reaching us in Spirit. If she had naintained all her physical faculties, it is likely that the expression of her physical ife would have involved her not being interested enough to seek my help and uidance. It was a delicate balance. Marjorie's soul actually chose to endure the llness she had before she was born. It was thought that this would give her the best hance of tuning into us for help. We did not want her to suffer so much pain as she lid. Some of this pain, I must add, was brought on by her attitudes, and her own egative thinking, in shutting us out. But on a deeper level, her pain and suffering reated a need and longing for love and healing of a type that she could not receive in he physical world, and so this helped ripen her to receive my presence.*

*You see, everything does happen at the right time, and you appeared in her life at xactly the moment when she was ready for our influence to become known to her.*

*When we were able to meet after her passing, she was not at first prepared to ccept me, but her stubbornness broke down quite quickly. She knew that I was there vaiting for her. Once she had recovered and orientated herself, we had many deep nd long lasting conversations. There was much for me to show her and to celebrate, ow that she was home. Of course, she was concerned for Reg and others that she ad left behind, and she sought my reassurance many times that he would be OK.*

*Provided that you have tried to love and do your best, not only for yourself, but or others too, it is likely that passing into Spirit after death is likely to be a happy xperience. There will be much for you to realize and learn about yourself, things hat you can only begin to know while you are in physical life. Your guides and piritual friends and loved ones will be there by your side. This is how it was for Marjorie, and now she is more settled and we have both begun to move on to further ields of learning and Spiritual progress.*

*When you die, you are united with your psychic ego, as I would call it, so that ou become a complete soul again. Into this soul, you bring the sum of all the xperiences that you have lived while on Earth in your most recent life that has just nded. When you have learnt lessons and gained awareness, your soul will then glow nore brightly, and radiate more fully, and be lighter and ready to rise to planes of igher learning.*

*Marjorie's soul has done this, and it has brought her much happiness and joy. Sadly, she will still need to return to Earth for further lives, because there are still essons that she needs to learn. But I believe that she accepts this now. It is very nlikely that her next life will be anywhere as physically painful as the one she has just left.*

*She is also looking forward to reuniting herself with Reg, when it is finally his time to pass over. There will be much for them to talk about and share. The love that two souls can share is so much greater on our side, and it is quite an indescribable feeling, especially for those as close as Marjorie and Reg, and there is much that they can anticipate when they are together again.*

**Session 4:**

It had been quite strange and challenging for me to try and allow Sojah to channel through me on the previous day. To do this with Marjorie had been much easier. I felt rather overwhelmed trying to tune in to Sojah. It was as though his being was massive and my mind was too restrictive to let him in. Inside me, I had felt tense and a little fearful, but I had been determined to do it. I had felt that I was able to convey a reasonable amount of the thoughts coming to me. Clearly, I was not as competent or gifted a channel as Marjorie had been, and I was rather afraid that I could be influencing what I wrote via my own thought patterns. Within me, I had the vague impression that there were things that I had missed or that I was not open enough to register. Yet, I felt that I had to persevere, and so, I was ready to go on.

As I prepared myself for this final session, I sensed that Sojah would want to talk with me again, and I wanted to relax more so he could use me as a channel with greater ease.

As I sat down to meditate in the sanctuary, I could feel a pain in the upper right side of my mind, like there was something much bigger than me that was trying to enter. I concentrated on my breathing to relax a little more. There were thoughts imprinting themselves upon my mind. It was Sojah.

*Paul, I am trying to reach you, trying to speak with you again today. I am here with you. You need just to relax and let me speak.*

*Paul, the work that you are doing is very important and very valuable. I would like to talk about the journey of souls through life. In channeling with you, I am trying to use your mind and the thoughts that you would have, so what I say will be expressed differently from how I would speak with Marjorie. She could put herself aside more completely than you. But the thought structures, outlook and beliefs in your mind are different from how they were arranged in Marjorie, and so I will try to light up and stimulate thoughts in your mind to express what I wish to convey and teach. There are some aspects of my being that Marjorie could channel more easily, and there will be other facets of my self-expression that you can pick up.*

*As I said yesterday, Marjorie's soul is now largely content. She was essentially successful in meeting her main life challenge. But there were also mistakes that she made too. So it is with all human beings. Marjorie became quite bitter and angry in the later stages of her illness, and this affected the degree of pain and suffering that she had to endure. If she could have remained more open to us, and our influence, she could have received a considerable degree of relief from her symptoms and felt a sustained level of peace. As much as we wanted to help her, she needed to reach out and accept that help. Often, when she was in greatest need, she shut herself off from us and put barriers in her mind so that we could not reach her. She knew that she was doing this, but in her mind, because she wanted to hasten her own death, she thought that this would be the best way to achieve these aims. When she shut us out, on the surface of her mind, she was able to doubt that we existed, and she could consider that it was all in her imagination. By generating these thoughts, a lot of confusion arose in her mind. And when she could not bring about her death as quickly as she wanted, then this created a depression where she became even less open to our influences.*

*Now that Marjorie is free, she knows how foolish she was with this behaviour, but it was a very tough test for her. At the time, she did what she felt she had to do to cope. The illness itself, affected her strength and ability to act constructively. She is just glad now to be out of that.*

*Many of you on Earth, suffer from illness, injuries or mental conditions that are very painful and difficult to bear. Sometimes you may wonder where it is that you can turn to, to receive help. You might get angry with your loved ones, like Marjorie did with Reg, just because you have to vent the frustration you feel inside. But I want to say to you that we are here to help you. If you can turn to us and ask for Spiritual love and help, we will be there and come as close to you as we can.*

*If you can imagine yourself with a peaceful presence surrounding you, some of you may be able to visualize the colour blue or violet and feel the deep energy of love and peace coming with this.*

*As much as you can accept the peace and love that we can bring you in the midst of your despair, you can start to feel that there is a reason to go on, and something to live for. When you finally come over to our side, you will be rewarded for your efforts, and recognize what a difference these times of reaching out for Spiritual help made to you.*

*Sometimes, souls choose a situation on Earth where they are likely to suffer, so that they will be encouraged to reach out for Spiritual help. From the depths of suffering, there can emerge a great wellspring of love and healing. We are always there, if only you can open your inner doors and seek for us.*

*For most things that you experience, there will be a reason for this, but human beings often make situations more tangled and complicated than they have to be. You need to find the path that wants to go forward in your life, but try not to be deceived that you are on your own.*

*There are many people in your world today that suffer acutely from loneliness, cut off from the comfort of companionship and feeling unable to share themselves with others. This is something that people create for themselves through their own thoughts. When you do not love yourself, others will find it difficult to love you too. You are all connected with vast patterns of love. The reason that you do not feel that connection is because you are self-absorbed, and you have put up barriers inside yourself to keep others out and to lock yourself away.*

*You do not need to be with huge numbers of people to find peace and to feel content with yourself. Human touch and loving words coming from one or two people can be a great source of comfort, but that contact will not solve your problems if you believe essentially that you are on your own.*

*We in Spirit know that love is at the heart of the universe. We are striving to bring that love through us in ever-finer degrees.*

*Love means for you to care for others, and indeed care for your self. In your world, that means caring for other human beings and all forms of life that you encounter. You might find that to be quite hard in the society that you have created. Often, the difficulties in your world are there, because you, as groups of human beings, have designed them that way. With your fears and beliefs that you are isolated and under threat, you have created structures and restrictions in your world that generate a lot of suffering. Greed and jealousy that you have not got enough, creates imbalances, so there is not enough for some, and more for others.*

*But these are physical things. Inside, if you can meditate, you will know that there is peace, and that nothing essentially can harm you. We are close by to help you, even if physically you may suffer and have to endure much that seems very hard.*

*Each time that you are able to care and open yourself to peace, especially in the moments that are most challenging for you, it is at these times that your soul will grow and learn a little more. From these experiences, you will find rewards in the afterlife, once you have passed over and joined us on this side.*

*My work with Marjorie, in this phase, is nearly over. I would like to thank you, Paul, for taking the time to channel my thoughts for the people to read. We send our love and blessings to you all.*

# Chapter 10 – Acquiring wisdom and acceptance

In our modern society, we value youthful vitality, health and well-being. Some of us go to extraordinary lengths to try and preserve a sense of being young and active. We exercise, try to eat wholesome foods and spend much of our energy to maintain a healthy lifestyle. Many people are very concerned to present an image of being young in front of others. There are television programmes devoted to helping people take steps in their lives so that they can appear to be younger than they actually are. This can include surgery to remove wrinkles and sagging skin, styling and dying hair, attention to clothing to disguise unwanted bulges and ungainly body shapes, and many other manipulations to assist one's self image. Underlying this are efforts to ensure that others will judge us positively and not negatively. It is as though signs of getting old are like threats to our self-image, something to be avoided, as much as possible, at all costs.

Our appearance and physical body is just the outer shell of who we are as souls. It is true that we have a responsibility to care for our physical self and give it love, because it is an essential part of us. However, a pleasing and beautiful physical body does not necessarily equate with a beautiful soul. There are numerous people who look very attractive and yet they are selfish and self-absorbed, unhappy and ill at ease with themselves. They might look nice but behave in a manner that is very uncaring towards others. If we are concerned only with the outer appearance of a person, then we will be blind to the soul. I believe that this is one of the main challenges of our modern age, for us to look deeper than the outer appearance of things, and search for the true beauty and meaning of what lies within us, and those with whom we associate.

In a Spiritual sense, youthfulness is just one aspect of human existence that we need to learn about through experience. It can be exciting for us to feel we are reaching out, expanding and improving ourselves. However, coupled with bursting activity, there is the need for us to experience passivity and receptivity, so that we can listen as well as act. With every new boundary that we cross, there is also the need for us to accept the limits of what we can accomplish. In trying to retain our youth, we can generate frustration and despair for ourselves, by trying to hang onto to something that we cannot keep. Our physical bodies do get old and worn out. That is how we have been made. Eventually we die, and we have to let go of that which we have tried to preserve, whether we like it or not. We can struggle against this process if we wish, but it will not bring us happiness. Certainly, we can enjoy the energies of youth while they flow through us, but when they diminish, the only way that we will find peace is through acceptance.

Marjorie was a person who had a great love of physical life in all its aspects. She was concerned about her appearance, but never excessively vain. All she wanted to do was to get out and about and express her self, as most of us do. Then, for the last twenty-five years of her life, she had to endure a relentless, ravaging illness, Rheumatoid Arthritis, which progressively stripped her of all capacity to act independently in the physical world, whatever she did to try and stop it. Added to that, the illness brought with it pain, that made living very unpleasant indeed. Her body became deformed, and in her own mind, quite ugly and unattractive. At times, she was very despondent about that. Physically, her body was a wreck. She could get very little satisfaction from it. While Marjorie focused on her physical self and tried to achieve what she could with that, she could find less and less meaning and purpose to her life. Her body was letting her down. Marjorie found her peace and sense of well being through her connection with Spirit and the work she did with Sojah.

When I looked at Marjorie, her body appeared very frail and hunched. Her bones were misshaped and very fragile. In conventional terms, she was not attractive to the slightest degree. But when I looked into her eyes, there was love and kindness that shone out from deep inside her. This was the love of her soul. People were attracted to that, and enjoyed very much to be with her. Marjorie's Spiritual learning was about moving from a place where she was fully occupied with the physical world to where she could focus on the soul and Spirit. Her illness was the catalyst through which she could do that.

Not everyone has to bear as much suffering as Marjorie faced, but there are some that do. It is very unusual for people to be immune from some degree of suffering, either to themselves or someone very close to them, during some phase of their lives. There are people who believe that any amount of suffering is fundamentally unnecessary, and efforts should be made to eliminate it from our lives. Drugs can be used, of course, to alleviate the excesses of physical pain, but suffering can sometimes have an inner meaning to it that needs to be acknowledged if we are to learn from it.

In Marjorie's case, the pain and loss of her physical mobility propelled her to look in other directions to fulfil her need to be at peace. The tranquility she felt when she received Spiritual Healing or meditated to go on inner Spiritual journeys was like a magnet to her, and she knew that opening to this was her path.

When we suffer from an illness or some form of loss, then this forces us to slow down and stop being active. On an emotional level, when we suffer, we feel the need to give attention to whatever problem we are facing. We might try to override that with our will, but suffering will compel us to shift our focus, sooner or later. Suffering induces in us a state of passivity rather than activity.

We can observe our usual activity in a different light, and are placed in a situation where we are no longer so involved in what we normally do. This gives us an opportunity to learn through listening within to our needs. It is in this more passive state that we can open ourselves to Spiritual revelation, where we might realize deeper patterns of what is going on in our lives. While we open to this more restful accepting state we can also gain inspiration and wisdom to help us move forward and grow. And so suffering has a value and can be potentially very important on our path of learning as a soul.

We might not welcome suffering and feel that it gets in the way of us doing what we want. When we do suffer, either from an illness or difficult circumstance, we can try to apply our attention to getting better and overcoming that suffering, eliminating it so that it won't bother us anymore. In so doing, we may miss the opportunity for learning that is there within the suffering itself. Nature has its own ways of assisting us to learn our lessons though. If we do not learn the first time, then nature will probably bring some further suffering to us at a later time, to determine if we are more receptive.

I have had many people come to me for therapy following times of crisis in their lives. Sometimes people have lost someone very dear to them, or experienced some dramatic change of circumstance, the kind of events that shake our sense of inner security. These critical moments can bring about an experience of feeling like we are at the crossroads in our lives. We can react negatively and fight against what is happening to us, or reach a point of acceptance that will prompt us to question and search for meaning in the unfolding of our life in ways that we haven't done before. It can be at these moments that we have important choices to make, and we need help to find our path forward. Patterns of our living, including habits and routine might no longer work for us and we could feel that we have to find a new fabric for our lives that will serve us more strongly and truly.

Some people do not like to suffer, and can feel afraid that it is a form of punishment for things that they have done wrong. Activity can be its own form of escape so that we do not have to face up to the kind of life that we have created for ourselves. People can make themselves very busy so they won't have to think about the areas of their lives that disturb them. Because we have free will, we might not like all the things we do or have done, and struggle to accept ourselves. We may make decisions and feel driven to act in ways that compromise our integrity and what we feel with our instincts to be right, and so we feel guilt and foolishness. Our assessment of ourselves may not be very realistic. But it could still feel easier for us to hide from ourselves rather than try dealing with problems and limitations with our outlook. Times of crisis then will feel very threatening to us until we feel ready to face more honestly our inner conflicts and wounds.

When Marjorie made contact with her guide, Sojah, he acted like a conscience to her, challenging her to become more honest with herself about areas of her life where she felt concerns. She did not always feel inclined to listen to Sojah because she decided that some of the difficulties she faced were too much for her and she did not feel brave enough to deal with them. When she did reach out for his help though, Sojah was able to comfort and support Marjorie and she felt a lot more peace.

With youthful exuberance, we can feel confident that we know what we are doing in our life and everything is going to plan, but then we can be shaken by events out of our control, to help us realize that we do not know as much as we thought we did. This is where faith can be important. With faith, we will trust that each circumstance in our life is being guided for us to learn our lessons and for us to grow as a soul. We will open to receive the blessings of each day and feel happy with that. However, this is a state of grace that even the most spiritual of people will be challenged to sustain all the time.

Marjorie struggled to maintain the faith that her illness was something that she had chosen. Deep inside, she knew that it was so. For much of the time after she contacted Sojah, she did endeavour to make positive use of her Spiritual gifts. She managed this in spite of a large degree of physical discomfort. However, Spiritual faith does not come easily, and we can all be tested quite severely whether we can retain it or not. Marjorie had her own tests, and this became more apparent after she stopped hosting the Healing group that she had helped to establish. It was then that she increasingly questioned the relevance of having a Spiritual outlook in her life.

Our soul has its own agenda for us, and if our soul has decided that we want to learn a lot of Spiritual lessons during our lifetime, then our life will probably not be very easy. Events will manifest in our lives to test and challenge us repeatedly around certain aspects of our character until we learn those lessons and are ready to move forward. The tests will involve whether or not we listen to inner promptings about what we need to do and act upon that, or rather follow our appetites, desires and direct ourselves to do what we want, regardless of what our inner conscience is telling us. Our fears can be the biggest obstacle to us being true to our Spiritual path. When we feel fear, we will want to stay where we are. We will not want to change, or to move forward; we will want everything to remain, as it is, where we can be safe. The thoughts in our fears will prevent us from growing as souls. Love can overcome fear. When we feel fear, we need to ask deeply inside, what is really true.

We can veer away from our Spiritual path through choices that we make with our will. When this happens, we will feel unhappy or at the very least, vaguely unsettled. As we learn our Spiritual lessons, we will become more sensitive, and any deviation we make from our true path, we will feel more acutely. This unease will result from the fact that our actions are going against the needs of our soul. We may try to cover this up with our thoughts and pretend that we are OK, but deeper inside, we will know otherwise, and this will produce a pressure inside us to change. As our lives unfold further, we could continue to make decisions that take us further and further from our true path, and out of fear, we might refuse to listen to any suggestions that could help us. Eventually, this can lead to destructive or self-destructive behaviour and it will be hard for us to cope with decisions that we have made.

Sometimes, we need to make mistakes in order to learn. If we feel unhappy about a decision we have made, we can feel bad about ourselves or possibly blame others for what has happened, or more constructively, we can seek for insight that will help us make better decisions next time.

Many of the Spiritual lessons we all have to learn involve loss. Marjorie's guide, Sojah, has reminded us many times, that when we die, we have to leave everything behind except our consciousness. There is nothing of the physical world that we can take with us.

In our youth, especially, we form strong attachments in the physical world. These include material possessions, relationships, physical health, home environment, and all sorts of things. Attachments are important to us, because by wanting something very much, we activate our love on the physical level, and we need to do that to be living our physical lives to the full. In the early stages of our life, we learn through the experience of gaining involvement in the physical world. Then as we get older, and our capacity to act in the physical world is reduced, we learn by letting the importance of that go. In our maturity and old age we are gradually prepared to die.

From the channeling of Marjorie's guide, Sojah and my studies of near death experiences and past life deaths, the transition of leaving our physical body when we die is often an ecstatic occasion. When the time is right, the experience of dying can actually be very joyful. Sojah taught us that death is a homecoming to that place of Spiritual love where we truly belong. If we open our hearts with positive expectancy as we approach death, then this can help our progression of gaining Spiritual awareness tremendously.

This teaching can be very hard for us to fully appreciate while we are in the midst of physical life. We build up our sense of identity around our close relationships, our home, our work, our possessions and habits, the environment where we live. Most strongly, we identify with the functioning of our physical body. Where any of that changes for us unexpectedly or is taken away from us, we will be challenged as to how we cope. We will question about our inner security and what we can rely on, and where we can find meaning for what is happening to us. Instinctively, we will reach out for guidance and support, or else retreat through fear and build up a shell around us to try and protect us.

Lots can change for us as we get older, but our capacity to love does not diminish with age. Nor does our ability to reflect and gain understanding from within us. Traditionally, in tribal societies, the elders of the community have been the keepers of the wisdom, the ones who, through experience, could guide the younger ones to learn to value what is truly important.

When we had our healing group, Marjorie would sit in her armchair in the middle of the room. Even when she wasn't channeling, others would turn to her as the wise elder for advice. Here was a woman that was crippled and could hardly do anything physically for her self. Yet, she was the one that the others recognized as having a deep connection with Spirit, someone therefore, who could help them find out what was important in their lives too.

When we observe life, we can see that our human existence is ephemeral, and physical life is in a state of flux, so that nothing in our material world remains permanently. The only energy that we can rely on is love, and this is what exists as the eternal foundation of our life. We need to accept the physical world for what it is, and interact in it with as much integrity as we can. Even when everything else is stripped away, there is still love, provided we can open to it.

As human souls, we are learning to experience the fullness of love in all its aspects. Our human existence is the educational faculty from where we are tested and learn our lessons.

Marjorie had her share of tests and challenges while she was alive. She had strong and loving Spiritual forces working with her, and once she became conscious of them, she was able to channel them in service to others. She had some wonderful moments where she could experience great love and the marvels of Spiritual life. In some aspects, she faltered, and her fears and limited thoughts blocked her from reaching her potential. Her greatest gift is the Spiritual teachings she was given that remain as a legacy. In other respects, she was a fallible human being on her journey as a soul, just as we all are.

# *Part 2 – The teachings of Sojah*

## Chapter 1: The journey of our soul

Over the years, Sojah expounded a Spiritual cosmology and outlook to life that was coherent and consistent. Sometimes, he gave discourses on particular themes that he felt were important or relevant. At other times, he revealed his thoughts through questions that he answered from people who sought his advice. Because Marjorie required my help, I was present for nearly all the public channeling sessions that Sojah did. There is also a wealth of transcripts from various sessions of his teachings that I have been able to study. From my knowledge of his thoughts, in the following chapters, I would like to present my own interpretation of his essential teachings. Some elements of these have been outlined earlier in the book, but here, I would like to go into more depth to describe in detail what I feel that he wished to convey.

In this first chapter, I would like to express what Sojah purported as our overall soul journey with understandings from a Spiritual perspective about what this entails for us.

Sojah taught us that, at the foundation of all life, there is a supreme, loving being, a force or energy, that we could call 'God'. We carry the essence of that 'God' force deep within us, as does all life. As human beings, we use our will in a journey of discovery so that we can learn to express the energy of God ever more through our actions and way of being. It can take many lifetimes for us to learn this, and in between our lifetimes, we rest and integrate what we have gained from experience on earth. From humble beginnings, we grow wiser, and rise higher in consciousness, and eventually, we no longer need to physically incarnate. Then we further evolve until we become beings of pure light and love, fully attuned to the energy of God and choosing to be at one with this love and its manifestation.

We have an enduring essence that is individual and grows and matures as we learn to love and express 'God's' will. This essence is what we can term our 'soul'. The earth is one place where human souls can live and learn their lessons. It is by trial and error that people learn what is necessary for their souls to grow. People have to learn to accept the various conditions of life and the limitations that physical life can place upon us. When we incarnate, much of our soul remains in Spirit and connected to the wisdom and experience we have gained through our numerous incarnations. I wish to call that aspect of our soul, our Higher Self. During our physical incarnations, as we learn to listen within to our Higher Self and those forces and beings that are trying to help us from Spirit, we can advance and learn those lessons that are essential for us. When the aspect of us that is physically incarnated, our Personality Self or Ego, is in harmony with our Higher Self, then we will feel peace and be open to Spiritual influences.

People wonder what it is like when we die and where we go, and whether we need to be afraid. Sojah teaches that when our physical life is completed, we leave our bodies and rise up high to a place of great light and love. This is the Spiritual realm. The vibrations here are much finer than on the physical plane. It is a multi-layered place, fascinating and absorbing, a place where we will feel free and at home. The soul has its home in the Spiritual realm. Within the beauty of the Spiritual realm, there is a much stronger sense of the depth of God's love and we are bound to face the truth of who we are and how we are progressing on our Spiritual journey. There is nothing for us to fear here. We can just be fully who we are without needing to hide or protect any aspect of our self.

The process of death and birth are interlinked and form mirror opposites of each other in terms of process. From the base of the Spiritual realm, strands of our soul extend themselves into the physical realm by the process of birth, so we can live incarnations as human beings. When we are born into physical life those threads of our soul remain within us, but we are restricted in our consciousness. In normal circumstances, the process of birth needs strong will and intent so we can emerge through the birth canal into our world. Physical life is a place where we have to work and make efforts to be in harmony with God's plan for us, and the plan we have made as souls for our growth in the Spiritual realm.

Sojah speaks of a silver cord of energy that links the aspect of our soul in physical form with our Higher Self in Spirit. It is like the energetic equivalent of the umbilical cord that is so vital for us while we remain in the womb, except that the silver cord links with our greater soul being rather than our mother. As we approach our death, this silver cord weakens, and then when we die, it snaps and the consciousness of our personality self leaves the physical body and ascends to be reunited with our Higher Self in Spirit, bringing with it all the experiences it had gathered while in physical incarnation. The physical body, then, without having the force of soul to enliven it, quickly decays, and the matter comprising our body returns to the constituents from whence it came.

We are born into physical matter as independent beings, and with our free will, we choose our own unique path. As such, we can be as much creative as destructive. Before we are born into our physical bodies, our souls make a plan of what we want to learn and the experiences and how we wish to proceed. Once we are incarnated physically, we can either choose to go along with that plan and fulfil its purposes or not, according to how much we are prepared to listen deep inside of us as to what feels right and act on that.

When we are first born, we still carry some degree of that 'God' energy that we experience in our Spiritual home. We are used to love and feeling the harmony of life co-existing around us. It can be a shock to experience the lack of that love and harmony in physical life. This can be very painful and we can easily feel hurt. We have to adjust to it. Our parents, and mother, in particular, are guided to try and offer us that love and protection that we need, but they are not always successful or able to do it. Progressively, as our physical life unfolds, the Spiritual light within us will become somewhat hidden from us unless we seek for it and try to live truly so our light can shine. As we grow older, we have to learn not only physically, but also in a Spiritual sense, as well as we can, to stand on our own feet, and live the life that feels right for us.

There are Spiritual beings available to help us, if we turn to them. For most of us, it would be too much for us to experience physical life completely on our own. We would not be able to cope with it. That is why there are Spiritual beings that stay close by us even if we are only very faintly aware of them. When we feel peace at times of trials in our lives or promptings suggesting for us to act in particular directions, promptings that, when we act on them, turn out well, these can be indications of our guides and Spiritual helpers that are there and trying to support us.

Sometimes people believe that there is no help for them, and their heart closes down, and then they feel very alone and unhappy. In such a state, we are unlikely to be very loving or God-like and we might act in ways that cause hurt and pain to others. It is our challenge and trial then to find our way to 'God' and that love within us to enable us to feel more fully connected with our soul and the Spiritual plan we have chosen for our self.

We need many lives to learn our soul lessons, and with each lesson that we learn, our soul in Spirit becomes a little more mature and is able to expand to embody that consciousness of God to which we all ultimately aspire.

When our actions on Earth are motivated by thoughts and feelings that are not loving, then our vibrations are heavier and it is more difficult for us to unite with our soul and Spirit. Deep inside, we know the effect that our actions have on others, and when we return to Spirit we need to perceive and feel that fully. The tasks we set ourselves may not feel very comfortable and can demand a lot of strength, determination and faith for us to succeed. They are tests of character, and as we pass our tests and become conscious of what we have achieved, then we grow stronger. Many times, souls will avoid learning a Spiritual lesson, because, once we are in the physical plane, it just feels too difficult.

As we descend into physical matter and involve our selves in physical life, we gain awareness through our efforts. Our soul character develops as we meet situations honestly and express our inner soul qualities through our actions. We test ourselves through many various angles and perspectives of experience, learning to love and be true to our soul intention. It is an important component of our journey to make mistakes, because mistakes teach us to value approaching our life situations with care and respect.

We need to learn to accept that we make mistakes and forgive others and ourselves when this takes place. There is no such thing as perfection for us as human beings while we are on the Earth. It is a matter of doing our best in the situation that we find our selves.

Once our physical body has died and we have risen up to Spirit to be reunited with our Higher Self, there follows a process of evaluation about how we have fared with the lessons that we set out for our selves in that life that has just been completed. We might find that some of the lessons were accomplished and others were not. Then we will need to make plans with regards to the lessons that we have not completed. When we are ready, we will feel the need to try again to more fully learn those lessons in another life, although not necessarily immediately or in the next life, depending on what feels right for us to do. We will be mindful of the effect that our actions have had upon other souls and may feel that we need to balance and assist especially those souls that we have hurt or damaged in some capacity. There could be situations that we can set up for our soul in future lives where we will have the opportunity to put things right. With those lessons that we have accomplished, we will be ready to incorporate the learning of those lessons into our greater soul, and move on to additional lessons that we need to embrace to gain experience of further facets of life.

One of the central components of the Spiritual universe is a sense of balance and harmony. We will feel the need to be attuned as fully as we can to these elements of being so that we can be at one with 'God' and 'God's love'. When our actions, while in physical incarnation, stray away from the plan we have set ourselves, we will feel with our greater soul being, that we have to restore that balance and harmony, where distortions have occurred. Adjustments that we feel we have to make as souls to restore this balance is called our Karma.

Usually, when we make our soul plan for a forthcoming physical incarnation, there will be some components of karma in our plan, so we will be endeavouring to rectify imbalances that stem from previous incarnations. For example, if in some lives we had been over-aggressive, we might feel the need to experience a lifetime where we have to be passive or humble or where someone is aggressive towards us, so that we can learn to express the polar opposite qualities of aggression more fully and bring that dynamic into balance in our soul. There could be several options of how we could do this, and as a souls, we will have the choice of how we wish to proceed so that we have the best chance to learn our lesson. Karma can be connected to specific relationships with other souls, where these other souls will in most cases be involved in the balancing process. Otherwise, karma can also be related to general limiting behaviour patterns and then be linked with how the soul reacts to specific types of situations rather than being work with particular souls.

The soul plan we make before physical incarnation can also have other ingredients. We might choose to embark on a new situation and quality of experience in physical life that we have not tried before. By doing this, we will be expanding the scope of our experience as a soul. How we respond to that could broaden our learning and add to our soul maturity. Especially when we are at the earlier stages of our advancement as a soul, there could be many lives, where we basically need to explore further.

Whatever situations we encounter during the course of our lives, there will in all probability be some Spiritual meaning behind it, and if we can attune to what that could be, then it can help us to learn, and make the most of it. Sometimes, we just need to pray and ask for Spiritual help in order to gain insight or acceptance so we can go forward.

There will be Spiritual beings on hand to assist us, ones that are wiser than us and can help bring us insights to enable us to grow and bring balance and harmony to our being. Even in Spirit though, we have our free will and we are not bound by the wishes of others. We have our own unique path for which we are responsible, and it is our task to own that responsibility and learn to proceed wisely.

When we eventually learn enough of the lessons that are required of us on the physical plane, we can rise higher in our consciousness and gain further learning in the Spiritual planes so our journey continues towards being 'God-like' and expressing that through our being. We might then take on the responsibility for being guides for others and helping souls less far on their path than us, souls that are still learning their lessons through physical incarnations.

Although we are all souls on a Spiritual journey, not all souls choose to move forward at the same rate. Some souls may choose to spend much longer between physical incarnations than others and feel the need have a long rest in their learning process at some point. Others can become tangled up in some soul issue or problem where they keep making similar mistakes and find it very difficult to extricate themselves from this soul test. There might be some challenging lesson that we need to learn, but for whatever reason, we might decide to postpone that lesson and follow other tracks instead. We might decide to enjoy contentment in the Spiritual realm for long ages without going through any physical incarnations. Another soul may choose to densely follow one life soon after another so that it can hasten advances in its learning. If we make some significant mistakes in one of our physical incarnations, one soul will want to go into further lives to rectify those mistakes as soon as possible while another will prefer to wait. For some souls, the pain of physical incarnation can be daunting and they can need a lot of persuading to continue incarnating. Mostly though, souls will realize, that if they want to grow and advance, then they have to challenge themselves by living human lives and facing their trials. In the Spiritual realm, there is a tolerance and an acceptance for all souls to choose their own path.

There are many possible courses of interest that souls can follow. A soul can choose to specialize in some form of creative expression. For example, a soul might spend many incarnations becoming attuned to the vibration of music, and even study this in the Spiritual realms, so this becomes something that this soul can share expertly and offer the beauty of this to others. Eventually, that soul will still need to incorporate other elements of experience into their being so they can find balance, but they still could carry that love of music as an element that is intrinsic to them throughout their evolution.

There are many gifts and qualities that souls can develop. On a positive level, some of these could include leadership, healing, patience, diplomacy and a sense of inner beauty. Alongside of this, there can be less desirable qualities, such as greed, possessiveness, dominance and vengefulness that become prominent in souls. A soul may need to learn to transform tendencies towards greed by becoming aware of what is truly important and valuing that so that other acquisitions no longer matter. With possessiveness, the soul might have to realize that there is love for him or her, and hanging onto another will just restrict what we can receive. A soul with a tendency towards domineering situations could be facing lessons about appreciating self-worth through simplicity, that we all have an important place in God's eyes. By letting go of the desire to be important, we can appreciate our true worth so much better. Someone inclined to vengefulness will need to respect the sacredness of life. By hurting others, we will only be hurting our selves. If we are already hurting, we need healing, not to hurt others and make it worse for ourselves.

Other souls may find in themselves a tendency to withdraw and isolate their selves out of a fear of being hurt. It will be important for these souls to learn trust and to dare to open their hearts to companionship with other human beings.

We are not on our own during our soul journey. There are souls that we may choose to meet, over and over, in various diverse lifetimes. What draws us together will be the love that we share, a love that can grow through each experience. Love is a great attractive force, and it will be comforting to be close and support those that we love most. We could be part of a group of souls committed to helping each other learn and advance together. When we encounter a soul that we love very deeply in Spirit, while in our physical incarnation, then any lesson that we have chosen to learn in association with that soul, will be much more keenly felt than with a soul that is relatively new to us. When we engage our feelings at a deep level, the soul learning will be greater.

There could be a large circle of souls with whom we associate and maybe a core group of those where we feel particularly close. As we evolve and mature as a soul, the circle of souls with whom we are acquainted will naturally become larger. We might move through different circles of souls as our experience widens, and every soul we meet will have their own expression of love and individuality that can add to our learning. We can draw closer or drift apart from other souls as we proceed on our Spiritual journey and choose the direction where we want to go

Our soul love can express itself not only to those with whom we share physical incarnations. Sometimes we will become very close to that soul who is acting as our Spiritual guide, and be drawn to share further activities with them, as is appropriate for us. They might be able to take us under their wing, so to speak, for some parts of our journey, and the love of that experience will attract us to them. We can also feel a love bond with particular places where we have incarnated and wish to return there over and over again. There could also be souls from the animal kingdom that become very important to us, and the love bond we share with them will also draw us to them, and we might meet with that animal soul in a number of lifetimes.

Sometimes we can become too attached to another soul, and we may wish to be with them even if it is not conducive to our soul growth. It could be the familiarity that draws us. We might then need to release that soul somewhat to enable us to be less restricted in the focus of our attention. Then we can express the love of God more fully and reach our potential as a soul. This can be very hard if our desires are bound up around that soul where we want to be with them above all else. Ultimately though, we will not ever lose that soul. Once a love bond has been established, it will remain throughout eternity, continuing to manifest in various patterns as we evolve.

We can also acquire strong negative feelings towards another soul. We might feel hate or anger or jealousy towards another soul. Over a number of lifetimes, these feelings could remain and gather in intensity. With each new lifetime where we meet that soul, at a sub-conscious level we will feel the feelings from the previous times, and especially those emotions that have been unresolved from some previous source of conflict.

These emotions will be felt very differently when we are in Spirit and we will be aware of the essential love that is there between us. Then we might make plans to work out how we can resolve those recurring difficult feelings between us from our lives on earth where we meet, so we can find peace together. Sometimes those souls that we find most difficult can offer us the biggest tests for us in terms of us learning tolerance, acceptance, understanding and forgiveness. We might be tempted to react angrily to situations with that other person because of the inner disturbances that are there, when, if we listen deep inside, we would respond much more calmly and with greater respect for that soul and our selves.

There are many errors and pitfalls, we can encounter in our physical incarnations. A lot of these can stem from greed, where we want more than that to which we are entitled. Our desires can be very strong and demanding. The feelings of power when we are able to gather things or people to us can be very intoxicating. However, if we try to take something and it is not meant for us then it will not stay with us. Ultimately, when we die and leave the physical body, we cannot bring anything with us except our experience. We have to detach ourselves from all that we could call our own. And if we have not been kind, loving or respectful, then our light will not shine so brightly.

Sojah repeated many times that if we adopted the motto of trying to behave towards others, as we would wish others to behave towards us, then this would help us to achieve that balanced perspective we need to make progress on our Spiritual path.

Sometimes, if we had a lifetime where we hurt and caused pain to others, we might then, in another lifetime, in an effort to find balance, choose a life of service, where our plan is to dedicate our self to put the needs of others before our own, where we set out to help and act lovingly towards those that need it. A life of service could be one where we do good works in some humanitarian effort. It might also be, as an example, a life where we are born as a handicapped child where we need a lot of looking after and attention. The act of service then, could be to the parents who might need to learn a specific lesson of love and we are providing the means for them to do that. It can be very subtle. When our motivation comes from love though, whether on the level of our greater soul being, or from choosing to care for another while in physical incarnation, our actions will be rewarded Spiritually, and we just have to trust in that.

We can choose a life of service as a soul, even if there is no need to do so from a Karmic point of view. Sometimes, advanced souls, who have passed the need to incarnate will return to earth in a physical life because there are some souls they wish to help in some way through an act of service. Even if we are not so far on our path though, we can still choose to serve. Then, as we help others, we will be also helping our selves.

Our journey as a soul can be perceived as a fascinating adventure, one of great joy, one where there is so much more to learn and embrace than we could imagine. There is so much more to our being than what appears on the surface. It is up to us whether or not we want to learn about the Spiritual nature of inner reality. For Sojah, it was always very important for people to make their own discoveries and draw their own conclusions. The knowledge of his teachings gave indications about what could exist in Spiritual terms. We then needed to test this to determine in our own minds what we felt was true, and then build our lives upon that.

# Part 2 – Chapter 2

## The power of thought

Sojah spoke often about the fundamental nature of thought, not only how the thoughts we generate affect our lives as human beings, but also how the creative energy of thought manifests reality on the Spiritual planes.

Because we have free will, we choose our thoughts. Our thoughts are an energy that emanates from us and forms a component of that energetic field that exists around us called our aura. The aura is in a continual state of flux and movement as our thoughts and emotions change. At a subtle level of our being, others close to us will be aware of our thoughts because they are energy that mingles with our immediate environment. We cannot hide them.

When we link our thoughts with emotions and our imagination, this makes the thoughts more powerful and can contribute to us manifesting in some form, what we are thinking about.

If there is someone standing in front of us, we can have many different forms of thought that we might project, relating to that person. We can imagine how we could use that person in order to obtain something that we want, or we may feel threatened that they might hurt us and want to withdraw from them, or we could be occupied with other situations in our minds and just want them out of our way. We could also tune into their heart and sense the wonderful love that exists deep inside them and want to appreciate that or be close to them. The choice of what we focus upon is up to us. Thoughts that are loving, constructive and with a helpful intent are positive thoughts while those that wish harm, are critical or manipulative are more negative thoughts.

Positive thoughts will emanate an energy that is lighter, stronger and more radiant, while the energy of negative thoughts will be heavier, duller, and sometimes hurtful. Someone who predominantly generates positive thoughts will have a much more vibrant aura than another person whose main thoughts are negatively based.

In terms of Sojah's maxim that it is best for us to treat others in the way that we would wish to be treated ourselves, there is an implication with this is that whatever we put out from ourselves in terms of thoughts, will contribute to the manifestation of our circumstances and how we perceive that which we are experiencing. The principle of 'like attracts like' operates with regards our thoughts, so that whatever we put out is likely to return to us, in one form or another.

If we are unhappy about somebody and don't like something about them or what they are doing, then as we focus upon that which we don't like, or judge it as being bad, then we will be generating a cloud of negative thoughts around us.

This cloud of energy will then affect our peace and we will be less open to draw experiences of love and beauty towards us. This will be true regardless of what thought forms the other person is projecting from his or her own mind.

When we carry negative thoughts in our energy field, others can pick up on those thoughts, and might be inclined to express similar thoughts to us, because those types of thoughts are already in the atmosphere. Thus we may attract negative thoughts to us by virtue of what we express from within our self.

It could be that around a home or working environment, negative thoughts gather from various sources and form a collective atmosphere in the building. People might then easily slip into a pattern of being critical and judgmental of others and feeling bound down by the atmosphere of the thoughts around them. Sensitive people, even though they might not want to behave in this manner, could still find themselves affected by this. We do have a choice about what we think, but it can be more testing when others around us are being negative. The negativity can feed on itself.

The problem is that once a cycle of negative thought begins, it can perpetuate itself, and it can also produce a pattern in our mind where we expect particular people or situations to behave in a more difficult fashion, and consequently perceive that person or situation in a darker light than is actually the case. This opinion can become a fixed view in terms of our inner expectations. Our perception then will be coloured by our thoughts and form prejudices within us that restrict us, forming clouds of negativity around us, and attracting experiences to us that would confirm what we think.

Sojah often used to counsel people with problems by encouraging them to be more open and flexible in their thoughts, and break down fixed patterns that were there so they could become aware of alternative realities, and have kinder and more accepting attitudes towards others. His teaching suggested that if people were kind and tolerant towards others, then they would ultimately attract kindness and tolerance to themselves, as long as they were open to it.

If we are exposed to a negative environment, we might need time in nature or in meditation to balance ourselves so we can express more positive thoughts, and perhaps, make a difference.

If we allow thoughts of negativity to grow too strong within us, it will drag our energy body downwards in a form of depression. There could be problems with people or situations that are bothering us, but by dwelling on this negatively with our thoughts, we will be creating our own problems. It is an important challenge for us to deal with the situations in our life as positively as we can with our thoughts. Only by doing this will our aura shine brightly, so that we can approach our life with strength and optimism, and not despair.

If we become caught in cycles of negativity in our own thoughts, then one thing we can do is to perform an act of kindness towards another. By a gesture of love of this nature, even if we have to struggle to do it initially, this will help to break down the pattern of negativity in our mind and it will shift the focus of our inner attention. As soon as we do something kind to another, this does bring love into our heart and affects our energy system beneficially. From that loving gesture, we might then notice some beauty or positive element in the situation or person we were considering, that we had not noticed previously. Our aura then will brighten and we will feel happier and freer.

Another step we can take to help relieve negativity is to ask for Spiritual help in the form of a prayer. As we ask our guides or angels, or God to help us, this helps to open our Spiritual channels. By setting this thought that we want help from Spirit, it invites this help to come to us, and then we might notice, shortly afterwards, that we feel more peaceful and ready to get on with our lives.

We can easily create illusions in our mind through our thoughts. We can imagine things about others or ourselves that are not true, but if we believe that it is true, then it will form its own fabric of reality in our thought patterns and energy body. Deep in our hearts, we will know what is true, but we can deny that with our thoughts, without realizing that we are fooling ourselves, if our heart is closed. We can then decide upon beliefs that suit us and we will build our lives around that.

For instance, we might decide that we are not lovable and that nobody will ever love us. From that belief, we could build a life of isolation where we don't expect anyone to come close to us, and we don't really let others come close either. For anyone wishing to help someone with this pattern of belief, this can be very difficult. Such a person will not open to receive help because he or she will not believe that it is possible, so any efforts to assist that person are likely to be in vain.

We could also be in a relationship with somebody and decide that this person does not accept us and that we can never please that person. There could be patterns in that other person's thoughts to trigger this response, but as this pattern becomes more and more entrenched, it could prevent us from experiencing closeness with that person. We will stay distant from them so we do not feel hurt. Again, our personal beliefs will set up expectancy inside us that we then expect to be fulfilled, and that will be the nature of reality that we create for ourselves.

There are numerous limiting belief structures that we can set up within our own minds based on our thoughts about others, our world and ourselves. Where these do not fully correspond with what is true, we will be restricting our capacity to give and receive love and to express ourselves as fully as we could otherwise.

We can acquire limiting beliefs via our conditioning, from what our parents and other authority figures tell us, but mostly we will be generating these with our own will as reactions to events that take place in our lives,

As an example, if someone speaks to us very harshly, what matters in terms of the thought patterns we carry, is not anything to do with that other person, and what they say to us, but much more, how we react to that harshness and how we deal with it. We might be very affected by other people's cruelty and feel easily hurt if we are criticized. It is possible that we can blame the other person for being abusive towards us. By doing this, we will be building up our own negative thought patterns. Otherwise, we could also try to protect ourselves, and check inwardly what is really true. Sojah's approach in counselling people tended to be along the lines of helping the person to appreciate the difficulty of the situation, and affirming the worth of their efforts, and then encouraging a response of acceptance and tolerance wherever possible.

What we create with our thought structures can have an impact, Spiritually. The path our soul has chosen for us will be one where we are learning to love and making the best of situations that we encounter. When our thoughts are positive and our heart is open, it will be easier for us to be in harmony with the needs of our soul, and listen inwardly to what our soul is prompting us to do. If we are affected by negative thoughts and dwell upon those, then our energy body will close down and we will be less able to perceive what our soul needs. We could then make decisions that are contrary to our Spiritual path and become, to some degree, disconnected from our soul. Our actions will be determined by the expectancies of our thoughts, and if our thoughts are negative, we can easily make mistakes and our actions might not be as well formed and loving as they could be.

It is hard for us to avoid thinking negatively some of the time. We are human. Many of the challenges that we set for ourselves as souls are designed to test us whether we will react negatively and veer away from our intended path, or whether we can accept and deal with our trials positively. We would need to be very advanced as a soul to get it right all the time. It is more important that when we become caught in some negative responses, that we seek help so that we can learn how to work through what we have created with the inner state of our consciousness around this problem, and shift the energy of it. This can be quite uncomfortable for us to do, because a pattern of negative responses can be very familiar and be like a security for us. If we do not feel very strong in our life, then we will not want to let these responses go, and we might feel fear about this, and find it very difficult to trust that any movement on our part would make a positive difference. We might feel that it is better to stay in the misery that we know than venture forward into an uncertain reality that could be worse.

Our thoughts also have an impact upon the nervous system of our body. As we express thoughts that connect with fear, then this will stimulate our sympathetic nervous system and our instinctive response of 'fight or flight'. We can think thoughts that trigger this response even when there is nothing there to actually fear. Once adrenaline starts pumping through our body as a result of this, it will make it much more difficult to change our attitude until we can give space for our body to calm down. In this kind of situation, if we can deliberately think positive thoughts and repeat them in our mind, then it will gradually help us to relax and open again

We can have many complex layers of thought patterns operating in our minds. Only some of these will be obvious to our everyday consciousness. Spiritual learning is a process for all of us that can need a lot of patience, and we can best make progress by taking one step at a time rather than expecting that we will become enlightened and able to deal with all our problems straight away.

Our thought patterns can also be relevant to what we experience in terms of the death of our physical body. Usually, when we die, we move upwards to the Spiritual realm and experience a great sense of love, light and peace. It is possible then to sift through thoughts and determine what has been true and useful in the way we have built our life, and what has been not. Spiritual beings will be on hand to assist so that souls can then learn more fully about what is true and discard those beliefs that have resulted in distortions or have been illusory. Part of the task we have as human beings is for us to align our actions as well as we can with what we know deep inside to be true, and to be open to learn more. If we have lived a life where we have based our outlook upon thought patterns that were very different from our inner soul intentions, then we will feel that we have wasted that life and not learnt what we wished to learn. When we build up limiting thought structures that are very entrenched, this can continue after we have passed into Spirit.

For example, if we carry the thought structure that we are not lovable and that nobody will ever love us, then this pattern will remain with us when we die. When we leave the physical body, we will still believe this. We will be closed to Spiritual help. Instead of rising up into the light and love of Spirit, we might find ourselves in a dark place or one that is very grey. Because we believe that nobody loves us, we will exist in an energy shell that is tightly around us, and no one will be able to approach. We will believe that this is what reality is like, and that reality will reflect exactly the beliefs that we carry inside us. It will be what we have created with our thoughts.

In the Spirit realm, thoughts have enormous power. Thoughts enable us to travel from one place to another. If we wish to be somewhere or with some other soul, the thought of doing that will enable this wish to be accomplished.

Communication between souls takes place by thought in a process like telepathy. Energy vibrates in different frequencies in the Spiritual planes, so it is necessary for the vibrations of souls to be in harmony and of a frequency that resonates for communication to take place. The Spiritual realm is multi-layered, and it is largely the vibration and nature of our thought patterns that determines where we will be situated in the Spiritual realm. As we evolve spiritually, our thoughts will become more liberated and of a finer and more subtle vibration. Our soul will then be able to rise higher in the Spiritual planes. An advanced Spiritual being can adjust its thought patterns to meet and communicate with others not so evolved, to help them learn.

In passing over to Spirit from the Earth plane, we will be aware of an enormous shift in perspective and a vast increase in awareness as we are freed from physical life. The degree of love and light that is present and the feeling of being at home will also strike us. But our thought patterns from our physical life will remain with us as a residue until we have fully processed and evaluated the lifetime we have just left and only then can we be fully united with our greater soul.

Sojah spoke of a place called the Hall of Memories that existed in Spirit. Before we could move on to further stages of learning, we would need to visit the Hall of Memories following on from a lifetime. In this place we would be alone, apart from perhaps having a guide to assist us, and we would be confronted with all our actions, thoughts and feelings from that lifetime, and the effect that these had on others. It might not be very comfortable but it is an experience of truth about ourselves that provides indications of how we can move forward Spiritually. The process of evaluation in the Hall of Memories strips away any distortions of thought or bias in belief structure that we, as a personality, had built up during our lifetime and confronts the soul with a balanced and frank experience of our human existence and how true we managed to be in relation to the path we had set for ourselves. Sojah spoke about how souls could be afraid of entering this place, anxious about how they had fared in their physical existence. Some would be shaken afterwards by what they had experienced, and need to be comforted by other Spirits. Others would be happy and realize that their efforts were to be rewarded. There would be no escape from going through this process for a soul, although it could be delayed until the soul felt ready.

In the period before a soul enters the Hall of memories, they could live in a world of their own thought creation in Spirit, and remain there for long ages. The test for them in the Hall of Memories, would be to determine how much their own thoughts are real, and how much is illusory.

As souls, it is one of our primary impulses to learn what is true. It is a search that is fundamental to our nature. It is the impulse to discover fully about 'God'. We do this with our thoughts. In our physical lives, we explore to determine truth from illusion, and this search for truth is intrinsic to our life, beyond the physical, in the Spiritual realms too.

# Part 2 – Chapter 3

## The Spiritual Planes

Sojah often likened the progress of the soul to a process similar to a student going to University. As we learned our lessons, channeled more love, and completed our inner tasks, we would advance in our development as a soul, and rise higher in terms of our vibration, awareness and attunement to 'God'.

In each physical incarnation, there would be some threads of our soul setting out to experience life more fully and adhere to a soul plan that would aid our inner development. As we met our challenges, when we would leave our physical body, at the end of our life, then the learning we gain would be incorporated into the wholeness of our soul being and help the maturity of our soul to grow.

When we did not succeed in learning the lessons of our soul plan from a given lifetime, then we would be held back in the area of that lesson from continuing our development, and we would feel the need to try again in another incarnation to learn that particular lesson so that our development in that area could proceed.

Souls develop at different rates according to what lessons they decide to take on and how they cope with those. Each soul has its own unique journey, but ultimately the lessons we all have to learn have the same common denominator, which is about learning to love.

At the end of a given lifetime, our consciousness rises up to the beauty and light of Spirit. Then our soul will enter the Hall of Memories to be confronted with how well we have done in meeting our inner objectives. We might discover that we have exceeded our own expectations or that we have made some terrible mistakes, or somewhere in between. As we emerge from that Hall we will be rewarded appropriately according to our efforts and their outcomes. If we have done well, our soul may then rise higher and be blessed with greater awareness and new opportunities to express love. If we have not done so well, we will be aware of residues left over from that lifetime, and we will know that we have to clear those and rectify mistakes that we have made before we can go further. It could be that our souls can be rewarded in some areas of being for our achievements but not in others. Making progress is something that will bring us joy as souls. We will also be happy for those souls with whom we are close, when they advance further too. There could be incarnations that we choose where we set out to help others rather than focus on our own soul's needs, just out of love for these other souls and our wish to help them move forward too.

Sojah taught us that the Spiritual realm is a multi-faceted reality and that it exists as a series of Spiritual planes. Each plane has its own virtues and characteristics. As we are able to rise higher through the planes, we find that these realms become ever finer in their vibration, more beautiful and with a greater radiance of love and light. As souls, we thirst for that love and light, and in our soul nature we want to move higher and ascend through the planes so that we can experience that love and light more fully. However, we can only experience and reside in the higher planes when we have earned the right through our actions and experience to be there. Our own vibrations have to be ready and able to adjust to the energy of a particular plane in order for us to reside there. We can only journey into one of the higher planes if we are invited and accompanied by our guide, or a being close to us of sufficient stature, that can then lead us there. It is necessary for us to have gained entitlement to be in a particular higher plane before we are able to do so on our own.

Souls from the higher planes descend to the lower planes as teachers and try to advise and help those less advanced Spiritual beings to learn. These more advanced beings are noticeable by the degree of their radiance and the depth of their love and knowledge. In the Spiritual realms, it is very humbling to be in the presence of one of these Masters. It is clear to our perception then, when we are with a being that is more evolved than ourselves.

The plane closest to us is the plane that Sojah and other traditions call the Summerland. This was the plane that Sojah could most easily describe because it is the one that is most Earth-like. This is the realm in Spirit where most of us go when we leave the physical body. It is also the plane where souls visit generally if they have out of body experiences.

In this plane, there can be the appearance of things similar to how they are on Earth. There can be fields, trees, houses, rivers, mountains, cities, and places to learn and serve. However, in the Summerland, everything is so much more beautiful than our physical world, and it has a radiance of light. What we see and perceive there is composed of energy and exists in a form that is much more fluid than the solidity of the Earth plane. We can feel strong emotions in the Summerland, but the prevailing feeling will be love. Communication with others will be via thought, and we will be able to create and manifest quite openly by using our thoughts.

For instance, if we are on a mountaintop, and we wish to be at the foot of a valley that is far below us, we just need to think that we are in that valley and we will be there. We can also summon other souls to be with us or we can travel to them, by 'thinking' that we are there with them with our minds.

In the Summerland, we know that we are beings of light, but we can still dress ourselves and take on a human like appearance when we choose to do so. We can also have our own home, and arrange this home according to our tastes and desires, and have this as a place where other souls can come and visit us.

There can be gatherings of souls to accomplish certain tasks. For instance, there are healing halls where souls can receive Spiritual Healing from other souls that specialize in this. There are places of study where souls can learn and gain knowledge of soul. Also there are places for creative self-expression such as art or music, but creativity on this level is done directly through thought and feeling and not with physical apparatus.

Below the Summerland are worlds of illusions where souls can create worlds for themselves through their thoughts, but in these worlds there is no substantial connection with others. These worlds manifest what those particular souls want to be true. They can be quite elaborate according to what that soul wants to believe. Deep inside, that soul will know that they are deceiving themselves, but there will be a resistance in them to admitting to a greater awareness of truth. They will feel more comfortable in their imagination and sense of security to keep things as they are.

It could be that they want to feel that they are more important than anyone else and create a world for themselves that supports this. They might hold some guilt or shame about something that they have done, and rather than admit that, it is easier for them to pretend that all is OK around them. It is also possible that because of some religious conviction, that when they die, they create a world for themselves that reflects this.

In their hearts, souls will feel uneasy and isolated in these in-between worlds. Any light they feel will be limited, and eventually they will yearn to open up and to reach out for help so that they can move on. As soon as they do this, there will be Spiritual beings on hand to assist and they will lift upwards, into the light of the Summerland. Here they will be invited to broaden their perspective, and as they open their hearts, they will perceive much more truly, their inner connection with others, and their place in the Spiritual realms. It could be that these souls will need much healing and support from other beings before they can fully adjust to this and come to terms with whatever was the source of their discomfort.

Part of Sojah's work was concerned with those lost souls, those souls that had cut themselves off from their greater self in Spirit and become very isolated and alone through their fears and beliefs. Souls could deviate considerably from the path that they had chosen in Spirit, and some would find it very difficult to return to that path. They might believe that they are alone and that nothing matters except what they want to do from a very limited place in their consciousness. Although there could be many other souls and Spiritual beings waiting and wishing to assist, it would only be possible to help them when they were open to it. Sojah found that it could be very difficult to persuade souls such as these, that there was help available. Their fears of venturing into the unknown could keep them stagnant for possibly a long while. These souls would increasingly feel in a very lonely and dark place. Finally, from a point of inner desperation, the impulse would grow where they would wish for something different. At this point, there could be a change.

When a lost soul finally reached out for help and allowed itself to be embraced by the light of Spirit, there would be much celebration, because then, that soul could start to grow again and feel its wholeness.

Sometimes, souls will remain close to the place where their physical body has died and this will be the place where the soul will build their illusory world. They may have residues of emotions that they are unable to resolve, and so, they continue to project an atmosphere of this emotion in the vicinity of where they are situated. These will be the Earthbound Spirits that are sometimes referred to as 'ghosts'. They are basically souls that have lost their way and become stuck. Generally, these souls are very unhappy, and will welcome the opportunity when it comes, for them to be released from the situation they are in, and to travel up into the light.

If we find ourselves in a situation where we are aware of presences around us, it can help for us to ask for personal protection for ourselves. Then we can invite that soul's guides and Spiritual loved ones to come close to help that soul. We can urge that soul to open to that help, and let themselves journey to their Spiritual home in the light. The Earthbound Spirit might well pick up our thoughts. Often, we will feel a change and this will be all that is needed to enable that soul to move on and reunite with their greater Self in Spirit. When that soul becomes aware of the help that is there and the presence of their loved ones, there can be much happiness and gratitude. But the soul does need to be ready to accept help.

Even if there is some negativity around that soul it does not imply that they are essentially evil, and once they open to the presence of their guide or loved ones, their energy can transmute so they can move on.

There are darker planes inhabited by beings that will deliberately avoid the light, and choose instead to feed on the energy of others for their own sense of power rather than opening to the true light and love of Spirit. Sojah spoke often about how 'like attracts like', and how we needed to be careful, so that if we generate fear, hatred or anger either towards others or ourselves, then this could bring these darker entities close to us, and those lower entities would both encourage the negativity and feed from it for their own gratification. In situations where we withdraw from Spiritual help, then the light of Spirit cannot protect us so easily from these darker influences. When our heart is open though, and we ask for Spiritual help, we will be protected and darker energies will not be able to come near us. Sojah was very insistent that love was the strongest force in the universe, and when our motivation came from a place of love, we could not go far wrong.

In the Summerland then, for most human souls, this is where we adjust to life in Spirit after we have left our physical bodies. We can meet with the souls of loved ones that we knew in physical incarnation. It is possible that we will find that there is a group of souls that feels like our soul family in Spirit. This group could have different members from the physical family that we had on Earth. Yet we could feel very dedicated to this group of souls. We could find that we have connections with many various souls for different purposes. These can stem from numerous lifetimes that we have shared together, or even Spiritual work that we have undertaken with those souls. And it can be joyful to meet up with them again.

Some of the souls that we knew while on Earth may have reincarnated and moved on. It will not always be possible to easily meet everyone with whom we wish to associate. But even when reincarnation has occurred, some form of meeting can occur and we will know that with those that we genuinely love, we will never truly ever be separated from them, that love is eternal.

The souls around us could be at different stages of development to us. Some of them may need to travel down from higher planes in order to be with us. We will only find our place in the planes once we have been through the Hall of Memories and evaluated our progress and where as a soul we have earned the right to be. Here, we are united with our greater soul being. It is possible then that once we have been through this Hall, we are able to be in a plane much higher up than the Summerland, depending on our maturity.

While we are in the Summerland, we might need some time out to rest, in which case, we can gain nourishment from the natural energy environment that is there. We could also need healing and psychological help in order to resolve difficulties that we have carried with us from the life we have just left. We might also decide that we want to learn and go to places like the Halls of Learning where we can study about our history as a soul, the history of the Earth and many other Spiritual topics of interest.

As well as doing things for our own self-interest, we could also decide that we want to serve and help others. We could choose a path in Spirit where we engage in healing, perhaps working in the Healing Halls or helping channel healing energy to the physical plane where people may be in desperate situations and have asked for help. There is also the Spiritual nurseries, where Marjorie's soul went, involved with looking after Spirit children and babies, helping them to grow and experience what they need so they can be reunited with their greater soul.

Sojah showed a vision to Marjorie once of a place where a vast number of souls were dedicated to sending energy and healing to the Earth, helping it Spiritually, to stay in balance and to be nourished, so that the fabric of life on the physical plane of the Earth could go on as well as possible.

There are many avenues of help where souls in Spirit can apply themselves and help themselves to grow and evolve in the process. Whatever souls give to others, they are rewarded for doing so.

Our greater Soul being could extend itself to various interests, but might also specialize and learn to grow through being dedicated to one particular activity and going into it in depth, and thereby gain respect from other souls with regards their expertise in that area.

For all the Spiritual activities in the Summerland, there are further dimensions of these activities in the Higher planes, except that the nature of the activities are on a subtler, more refined level. So, in the higher planes, there are also places of study and learning, self-expression, creation, service and love. All souls have guides and teachers, beings wiser and more advanced to help them to grow and evolve.

Sojah could not easily describe the higher planes in human terms, except to depict each onward plane as being more beautiful with a greater dimension of love than the one before it. The planes, themselves, extended ever upwards towards an experience of pure love and energy that is 'God'.

In addition, during the course of his teachings, Sojah suggested that there are many worlds beside our earth where human souls can learn and grow, other planetary systems in physical reality, and worlds that exist on other planes of reality. There are also many kingdoms of life besides our own. Included is the animal kingdom where animal souls will incarnate and continue to evolve in animal form. There is the plant kingdom and Spiritual beings called devas that work directly with the plants and the Spirit of the Earth. Sojah spoke about the Spirit within trees, that trees could be places of great peace, helpful for us to connect with Spirit, that trees could be very protective and comforting presences.

Altogether, the Spiritual universe is a vast multi-dimensional reality that we can only begin to understand with our human consciousness, even with all the teachings that wise beings, such as Sojah, can offer.

# Part 2 – Chapter 4

## Our Spiritual guides and teachers

One of the central planks of Sojah's teachings concerned the existence of Spiritual guides, wise and loving beings that work with us and support us while we are engaged in our physical incarnations on Earth.

During the time that we are still in Spirit prior to our physical incarnation, we make plans of what we wish to achieve in that coming lifetime. Generally, the main elements of our plan are in consideration of areas where our soul needs to develop to become more mature. We choose a path for our lifetime where we will encounter challenges to widen our experience and our capacity to love, as well as discover aspects of existence that we need to learn and assimilate. Through consideration of the body that we will inhabit, from our soul's perspective, we will be aware of aptitudes and inclinations that we are likely to inherit with the genetic makeup of that physical body. These attributes become the vehicle through which we express qualities of our soul. On a soul level, we will be mindful of the nature and patterns of conditioning we are likely to receive through interaction with our parents and the family that we would be born into. There could be other souls with which we make arrangements so that during the course of our physical life, we will meet them and have to work out our relationship with them in some way.

For example, we might choose a very difficult family circumstance as the base for our incarnation, one where there is a great deal of repression and maybe even abuse. We could ask ourselves why would we possibly choose a situation like that? It could be, though, that our aim as a soul is to find acceptance and forgiveness for hurts and pain that we receive, as a means for us to learn to love more fully. Such an aim might be very difficult for us to achieve, but ultimately very rewarding for us if we can manage it, and we might need to turn to Spirit and open ourselves to a lot of help in order to succeed in this. There might also be gifts of patience, courage and inner strength that we can gain as we attempt to cope with the challenges of this difficult upbringing. On a soul level, family members that are very challenging for us, might actually be there to serve us and give us the opportunity to learn Spiritual lessons.

If we do not achieve our goals with these soul tasks, and stay true to our intended path, we may acquire a lot of bitterness and anger in ourselves that we later project onto others. When we return to Spirit after such an experience, we will realize what we have done, and know, if we were not successful, that we did not learn the lesson we had set for ourselves, and we would then feel the need to tackle that type of learning situation again, to do better, as well as having the need of making up ground with the souls that we had hurt during that lifetime.

Quite often, there can be a lot at stake with the lessons we choose. If we do not succeed with a soul task that we have set ourselves, it can bring about the imprint of limiting behaviours in connection with our reaction to particular circumstances, from how we dealt with a challenge in a particular lifetime. These are then limitations that we then have to overcome in order to progress and open up to our potential. If we repeat the mistake in a further lifetime, the pattern will be reinforced. The tendency will grow in our soul to continue that behavioural pattern that is limiting us. It will become as a habit in our soul, something that is familiar, and it will feel more natural for us to perpetuate that limiting way of being than to do anything different. This is where we do need to be very strong to open ourselves to inner guidance. Otherwise, such patterns can become engrained in us for lifetime after lifetime and this will stunt our development as a soul.

In choosing the circumstances of a difficult family upbringing, there could be many options of what our soul chooses as a lesson that we hope to learn. Our soul aim might be more about us moving beyond the conditioning of our family and finding a measure of independence where we can express different and more humane patterns in our life than the ones that we were subjected to in our formative years. In this path, the learning might be more about asserting our strength of identity and independence as an individual and being able to withstand influences that would sway us from that.

It could be that we need to find peace with one of the other souls that are a member of that family, and we enter that family pattern with the specific aim of doing that.

There are many variations and subtleties with the path that we could choose that make everyone's experience quite unique.

We could also choose a warm and loving family environment into which we can be born. Receiving that love could then give us strength to deal with challenges later in our lives where conditions might not be so easy.

As souls, it takes us many lifetimes for us to learn all the lessons that we need to learn and acquire the skills and qualities that we need so we can progress. As our souls mature, we will be inclined to take on more difficult challenges, because we will need to master these to move further on our development.

During our physical incarnations, we will be encountering lots of different souls, at many different stages of development, all with their own agenda of soul learning. It will be our challenge about how we deal with those encounters that will determine how we move forward as a soul.

With our own soul development, we might have strengths and weaknesses. For instance, we might easily be able to open our psychic capacities and be able to help and heal others. But when it comes to close relationships, we might find it very difficult to trust, and be inclined to react very negatively if we get hurt. Because we are sensitive, we might find emotional hurts very difficult to withstand, and subsequently put up inner defences to avoid them, and therefore, become isolated from others. This pattern might persist through many incarnations. So then, in making our soul plan, we could be more inclined to choose a plan designed to improve our trust (our weakness) rather than further express our psychic capacities (our strength) as a means for us to grow and mature as a soul. The tendency for us, as souls, will be towards expressing our strengths rather than going into those really uncomfortable places where we need to learn.

In the main, we will choose a soul plan that is primarily aimed for our own development. Sometimes, we might put that to one side, and structure a lifetime that is designed to give an opportunity for learning to another soul that we love very much. We could also choose a path of service where we want to help many others through healing or teaching. This could be more for other's benefit than our own. These forms of acquiring selflessness can be a very important further step with regards to learning about love, and also help us on our Spiritual development. Alternatively, we might also be wishing to help others as a means to balance other experiences from our past where we have brought suffering to others, something we have to do in order to move forward.

To make our plan though, we need guidance. Even in Spirit, where our awareness is so much greater, it is difficult for us to perceive beyond our own limitations, where our development most needs to proceed.

So there are beings that are further along in their advancement as souls that can help us. The process of working out soul plans can be quite intricate and many factors can need to be taken into account, including our relationship with other souls that could be involved with us during our physical incarnation.

Those souls that would help and guide us, from Spirit, with our soul plans are ones that no longer need to incarnate in physical form, ones that have learnt already the main lessons of physical form. They are in a position to have a more rounded perspective of what we need. It is up to us whether we listen to advice that is given to us. Even in Spirit, we still have our free will.

There could be a number of Spiritual beings involved with us at the point where we are making our soul plans for a given lifetime, but there will be one chosen that would be our main personal guide for that lifetime. This guide will be one whose vibration and strengths are attuned to the qualities we need to express in that lifetime, so that as we come close to this guide, then this will help us to take necessary steps forward in our development.

It is probable that we would know the soul that is our guide. We might have met them in former incarnations. There would be some strong point of connection. But they will know more than us on a soul level, and there will be the possibility that we can learn considerably from them if we open to it.

Our personal guide will be mindful of the patterns of our development, and our soul inclinations, and will know us quite intimately. While elements of our soul enter into physical incarnation, standing alongside our Higher Self will be our personal guide, there to support us to make forward steps on our Spiritual path. There are many ways we can receive guidance to help us be true. By tuning in to the vibration of our personal guide, or by inner listening or prayer to God, or other Spiritual beings, asking for help sincerely, or by listening to what feels to be our conscience, we can then tread forward on the path we had intended for ourselves, through our lifetime.

During our physical incarnation, we need to make our own decisions. That is how we learn, even if we make mistakes. In terms of our soul development, we are like children learning to walk. Our guide will never take over from us, except in extreme circumstances. The role of our guide is to assist us to be true to our inner intentions, by being there, and being available on an inner level of vibration, if we wish for help, and to protect our space, as much as possible, from intrusions on a psychic level, that might not be meant.

As we descend into physical matter, our awareness is much diminished. Our capacity to perceive our guide or any Spiritual influence is much reduced. The possibility of our free will leading us astray from our path is very great. So we need to really apply ourselves if we are to be successful with what aims we have made in Spirit.

Some people, when they are born, retain some degree of sensitivity and can still sense Spiritual influences about them. Others are much less able to do this. It might be connected to a soul's plan for that lifetime about how much we are able to remain in communion with Spirit. It does not imply that we are less advanced as a soul because we feel less able to contact Spirit directly than someone else. There are different soul tests that we can apply to ourselves. Every aspect of our inner plan for a lifetime will be very personal and unique to our own needs.

Not everyone will be inclined towards wishing to communicate with Spiritual guides. Some, through their religious faith, might pray to 'God' and seek help for their life dilemmas with this highest source. Others may invoke the support of angelic beings, higher beings with qualities that can be channelled for the benefit of many, beyond the specific link that our guides have with our personal soul. Many people will not have any particular faith, and will just try to live their life as best they can, and rely on their instinct and intuition to lead them forward.

As far as Sojah was concerned, it did not matter which Spiritual orientation people had, as long as they were sincere, and reaching for truth with their hearts.

When people are open minded and trying to be honest with themselves, then the love and light of Spirit can draw closer, and our personal guides will be there, assisting us, whether we recognize them as such, or not.

Our Spiritual guides might not be the only Spiritual beings close to us. There could be angelic beings working with us, if we have asked for them. We might have associations with other Spiritual beings that have qualities that we need. These beings come close to us when we are ready to express those qualities. There could also be souls that have passed over from physical form, souls that we love, that want to communicate with us. These souls might have strong desires where they wish to continue their association with us. Those desires will naturally draw them to us and we could perceive their presence through our dreams or in our thoughts and awareness of what is around us.

Our personal Spiritual guides will be knowledgeable and equipped to help us with the fulfillment of our soul plan. If we are sensitive to Spirit, we will be able to learn to recognize them as a very loving and wise presence, like an extremely close friend, one that is there for us to support us, not on a physical level but on an inner level, and is basically there for us whatever we do.

Our guides can be quite passionate beings. They will have their own strong qualities and modes of expression. All Spiritual beings have their own journey and are seeking to become closer to 'God'. When we have a personal guide assigned to us, this Spiritual being has its own contract with us, and will be undergoing its own process of learning and unfoldment. As we are successful in living out our soul plan, and our Spiritual guide is able to help us appropriately, then they will be rewarded and be able to move further on in their path too. For our guides, there are also tasks about how they can best attune to us, and bring their influence to bear without interfering in our decision-making. They can learn and advance, even if we are not successful. However, because of the love our guides feel for us, they will feel joy or sadness with us, depending on the outcome of a particular lifetime.

Our guides will also be guided by higher beings, and can seek advice themselves about how they can best proceed in given situations. If a soul in physical incarnation is struggling with some awkward trial, there might be various options of how a guide could act from a Spiritual sense to lend assistance. This is where the guides need to tune in to what would be most wise and beneficial for the soul concerned. The guide may need help, themselves, to do this, especially if it is a type of situation that is new to them in terms of guiding.

So the process of learning continues right through the strata of the Spiritual planes, and is not just limited to our experience on Earth.

It sometimes occurs that our Personal guide can change during the course of our lifetime. This happens generally because some phase of our learning as a soul has been completed, and some other Spiritual being is more suited to help us with their vibrations, so we can open up to the opportunities that need to present themselves for us to go further.

For instance, we could have been going through our lifetime being concerned with 'normal' interests such as relationships, home and career, and then reach a point where there is the opportunity to adopt a more consciously Spiritual path of service, where we open ourselves more fully to gaining inner awareness, and placing ourselves in 'God's hands' for how our life is to proceed. This might be a time when, either, we will become consciously aware of our Spiritual guide and this will enable us to transform our life, or our actual guide will change, so a new guide will be there for us, one that is better suited to assist us with furthering our Spiritual path, and the former guide that was protecting us while we were occupied with those more basic activities will step aside.

Starting on a conscious Spiritual path will not imply that our occupation with our close relationships, home, our interests and career will become any less important. They could become even more important to us. We will be viewing them in a different light, and we will be seeking to do what we are guided to do from within, rather than just relying on what we want to do, or what we feel we should do out of a sense of duty to some system that is in place around us.

When we reach that point in our life where we could change, and adopt a more Spiritual outlook, we might also refuse to do so, and feel that we want to continue what feels more familiar to us rather than do anything different. Then, the change of guide that had existed in potential might not take place.

In our life plan, there may be many options of soul learning, of what we can do. We might take up some of those possible opportunities and not others. There could be several moments of opportunities given to us when we can make an important step in our lives. We might refuse all of them, or only partially agree to certain changes. It is a matter of choice on our part, but depending on what choices we make, the pattern of our life and how if unfolds will be affected. This in turn can affect the nature of the Spiritual help we are able to receive. The whole process is in continual fluctuation on many levels.

There are many possible events that could trigger an opportunity for Spiritual development and awakening. For some, it could be the death of someone close to us. We might lose our job, or go through a divorce, or travel to a country we have not previously visited. Very often, it will be times of crisis, or events that lead to us questioning our values, where we could make some important decision to change. These times of crisis are usually arranged in Spirit beforehand. How we react to these situations will be up to us, and will determine the next steps on our path.

When people lose someone that they love very much, through death, the desire to be with that person can very often lead to Spiritual experiences, and create an opportunity for the one that is left behind to develop faith and Spiritual awareness. It is possible that on a Spiritual level that events like this are planned to give opportunity for inner growth and awareness for that soul.

For example, we might be in a very close relationship with somebody and that other person dies. We will naturally miss that other person very much. This situation could propel us to want to know what has happened to this other soul, and learn about Spirit so we can communicate with them and not feel so separated. The love in our bond with that other person then can be a catalyst for us to seek Spiritual knowledge and helping us to begin to live a conscious Spiritual path. Alternatively, it may feel very unfair that this person has died. We could decide to blame 'God' and give up in our lives and feel that life is not worth living anymore. It will be our struggle to decide which way we go forward, but the potential will be there for us to develop Spiritually.

If we have loved ones that have passed into Spirit, they may draw close to us by virtue of the love that we share with them. If we feel strong family ties, then we could feel these presences much more readily than those of our higher Spiritual guides. Because our departed loved ones are Spiritual beings still in the process of needing to physically incarnate, they will have less perspective upon what our soul needs to develop than our Personal guides, but can still provide a great deal of comfort and Spiritual love. For many, feeling the Spiritual presence of someone they love that has passed over, can give evidence of Spiritual reality that can help a person tremendously to develop their faith.

There could be other Spiritual beings aside from our personal guides that become prominent and close to our soul during specific phases of our lives. These might be higher beings that want to help teach us in some ways, or other beings that want to assist us in channeling healing to others. There can be many opportunities of learning for our soul, and we need to be open and follow our inner instinct and intuition to be open to these.

There will also be an ancestral link with the souls that have been part of our physical family in a given lifetime on Earth. There could be traits and qualities within this family system that have a binding effect for the various members of this system. On a soul level, this can be both supportive and also restrictive. The soul qualities of a family system can express both strength and limitation. In this way, a soul may choose to enter into a given family with the aim of breaking a limiting pattern from within that family, as a personal test for that soul, but also to liberate all those souls involved so that the ancestral threads of that family can move to a higher level.

In considering the existence of our Personal guides and other Spiritual beings that exist, what becomes apparent is that we do not exist in isolation. We are interconnected with all other beings, the people and other life forms with whom we share life on the physical planes as well as a myriad of Spiritual beings that exist on other levels of existence. As we honour our relationship to all these beings with love, this can fill our being with Spiritual light that we can then express, and will bring us a profound feeling of peace and meaning in our lives. It is our choice about how much we open to this truth, and about focusing upon souls tasks that are in front of us. With our Personal Spiritual guides, it is about acknowledging that there are those that know more than we do, and this is very humbling, and there are many gifts that they can give us. Through their help, we learn to face our own inner truth and deal with the trials that we as souls have set for ourselves.

# Part 2 – Chapter 5

## Opening our Spiritual awareness

In his teachings, Sojah was very concerned for people to learn about Spiritual reality. He emphasized that the Spiritual realm did exist, that people could connect with it, and that it was a potential source of great love and comfort. Sojah was interested for people to gain direct experiences of Spirit and to overcome their fears about it. As people felt the loving presence of Spirit in their lives, they would feel greater peace and harmony, a sense of well being that was deep and real. Also though, Sojah wanted people to understand about the nature of Spiritual reality as part of a global effort to bring the Spiritual and physical planes closer together, for the sake of our humanity and other life forms on our planet as well as for individual concerns.

When we met as a healing group, and we united with love in the Spiritual work that we were doing, the presence of Spirit energy could be very strong. In the room where we worked, the feeling of greater energies than our own acting with us was palpable. For some people, it was like heat and a feeling of peace that pervaded the space where we worked together. This strengthened our faith. When we united in our prayers and invocations and called on the presence of Spirit, the efforts of a group of us acting collectively felt very powerful. Members of the group also did these practices on their own, but consensus within the group indicated that there was a greater intensity for these when we acted together.

Sojah expressed to us that the best methods to connect with Spirit were through meditation, contemplation and prayer. As we invoked Spirit to be with us, we invited those energies to come closer to us, and this enabled us to be aware of the presence of Spirit working in our lives. We needed to value our own inner capacity to access Spirit.

When people first came to our group, they often had no experience of meditation or connecting with their inner consciousness. Sojah had to teach us simple steps that would enable us to do that.

He suggested with meditation, that we first of all closed our eyes and focused on our breath. Then we could gradually feel the usual flutter of concerns that occupied our busy minds become less dominating. Once our awareness began to slow down, we could begin to observe more peacefully, the inner workings of our mind, learning from within, how we function. This was the beginning of the process of meditation. It was a skill that we could learn and become more adept at doing with practice. We could also use a mantra to help us. A mantra would be some simple sacred word or syllables that would be meaningful to us. It could simply be a word such as 'peace'. By repeating that word or syllable inside our minds with our eyes closed, we would gradually slip deeper into our inner consciousness. With our intention and focus upon our breath, and perhaps our mantra, we could regulate our brainwave activity, reduce the level of its activity and become inwardly receptive. This would have benefits for us, because in doing this, we would feel very relaxed and rested. Problems that we worry about might seem a little easier to resolve. Whatever our beliefs, meditation could help us.

Sojah proposed other methods for going into meditation such as looking into a candle flame or concentrating on the inner third eye, but was not prescriptive about this. He encouraged people to use their instinct and intuition and find the method that would best suit them.

Sojah maintained that meditation could be far more than a stilling of the mind. He taught us that our physical body was a vehicle for us to express ourselves. Our brain was the physical vehicle for our thinking and creative mind. Once we were in a state of deep meditation, we could loosen our ties to the material world so that we were no longer confined to that physical body. We could experience ourselves as pure consciousness. From this place, we could open our awareness to other dimensions of reality, communicate with other beings, and even travel to these other dimensions of reality while our physical body rested. Rather than this needing to be something for us to fear, Sojah suggested that we welcome the opportunities that this deep state of meditation could offer us.

The technique that Sojah most favoured when he led us into meditation was for us to focus upon our third eye, that space between our eyes, the intuitive psychic centre in our being. For most of us, in our normal functioning state of being in the physical world, this centre is largely closed in its psychic capacity and instead, our perception is dominated by our capacity for analytical thought. However, in a meditation state, we can focus upon our third eye centre and imagine as if there was a curtain there that we could lift up. As we do this, our psychic faculty can begin to operate and we can receive visions and connect with the Spiritual realm. It can be quite subtle at first, and visions that are revealed to us might seem as if they are only coming from our ordinary imagination. But as we encourage inner perceptions to emerge, we can begin to have experiences that are far more meaningful to us.

Sojah encouraged us to believe that we could have psychic experiences and connect with our guides. As we actively imagined that we could do these things, then this would help us to get there. By aspiring towards goals of inner awareness, our consciousness can make adjustments to enable us to achieve our aims. In Spiritual terms, what we imagine is a key ingredient in what we are able to manifest. We need to honour our imagination and use it productively to help us.

Often, Sojah would lead us in meditations where he would invite us to lift out of our physical bodies. The process of consciously leaving our physical bodies is usually called Astral travel. He suggested that through our thought, we could consciously learn to direct our being independently of our physical bodies and that there were wonderful discoveries that we could make by doing this

There are many reports people have made about how they left their bodies when they suffered some trauma. The shock of trauma can loosen the physical ties of our energy system, and people can suddenly find that they are looking down at themselves and not in their body. These are often wonderful experiences that have a huge impact on people's lives, enabling them to realize that there is more to life than their existence in their physical body. Generally, when people have related about these out of body experiences, they have spoken of the great peace and freedom that they have felt while in that state. Typically, it has only been with reluctance that they would come back.

Sojah suggested that we could learn to consciously leave our body, through intention and deep meditation. By expressing this wish to our inner consciousness and asking our guides to help, we could gradually develop the skills for this to happen.

The first time it happens might take us by surprise, and if we do not accept it completely, we might then be jolted back into our body again. It often is the case that people try a little bit too hard with their will at first, and then need to learn to relax and be patient. Gradually, if we persist with our efforts and practice, our abilities to leave the physical body can increase.

People might experience themselves looking down on their body or the room that they are in, or even going further and travelling high in the sky and beyond that, to other parts of the world. We might find ourselves drifting upwards and entering into the realms of light and Spirit, and having visions of beauty, wonder and love. It is not always possible for us to control these experiences. They often just happen quite spontaneously, and we have to then go with them. There might be Spiritual beings we can meet and converse with them via telepathy. They could be our guides or souls of people we knew that have passed on. We might even be able to meet with the Higher Self of people we know, and work out some things together on a Spiritual level. Our guides could be there and want us to accompany them on some inner journey of learning and experiencing. There are incredible possibilities.

When people first realize that they are out of their body, it is a normal response to feel some fear, and then as a consequence, we would be jolted back into our physical body. Fear does that. It does need practice to build up trust. Sojah tried to assure us that this process is safe, and that we could ask our guides to protect us and support us. We will probably be a bit clumsy at first doing this.

When we have a clear inner intention, this can help us, and we can improve our skills.

People sometimes can be jolted awake from sleep and feel that they were somewhere else, without quite remembering where. Sojah suggested that in these instances, it is likely that the person was out of their body and engaged in some form of astral travel, and then returned very quickly. In our sleep, it is common for us to detach from our physical body and go on inner journeys. Many of us visit loved ones or our guides in the Spiritual realm while our physical body rests in sleep. It is the time when our inner consciousness can extend itself, gain additional experiences and receive guidance.

If we are interested to practice astral travel as a means of learning about Spiritual reality and for self-development, or helping and serving others, then there can be many benefits. When we become free of our physical body, we can then connect more fully with our Higher Self, and become aware of aspects of our true Spiritual nature that we would not easily perceive otherwise.

We might choose to leave our physical body out of love and a wish to help or serve in some way. There may be someone that we want to comfort, and our desire to do this will actually help us to inwardly travel to that person. Through having a motivation of love or service, we will more easily be able to let go of attachments we feel to our own physical body. Within our minds, we will be reaching out rather than just being absorbed in our own physical processes. This will enable us to be more in tune with the Spiritual realm where love is much more prevalent and finer, and will therefore help us lift out of our bodies and go where we desire to be.

Sojah said to us so many times, that 'like attracts like' and by practicing giving out and receiving love in our lives, we will not only become more Spiritually minded but can open our psychic faculties as well.

People can feel inhibited to do astral traveling because they are afraid that they could become lost or journey to the wrong place and that some harm could come to them. There were, in fact, a few instances in our healing group where people did travel to rather strange and confusing places and did not quite know what they were doing there. But Sojah would remind us that by thinking of our physical body we would return there instantly, and that was what tended to happen when people did this. The other thing that people could do in these situations was to call on the help of their Spiritual guide. Whether or not we were in conscious connection with our guide, our guide would be with us and available to assist us, especially if we asked for help. If we proceeded confidently though, the experience of leaving our body, in all likelihood would be a very positive one, and that is what we could expect.

It is a quest that many people have, to make contact with their Spiritual guides. There is a natural desire for any of us on a Spiritual path to want to make that as strong and clear as possible. Our guides are one stage beyond us, Spiritually, and they are there to help us and teach us if we are open for that. Sojah suggested that we all have a particular frequency of vibration in the way we interact with our environment. When we go into a deep state of mediation, then we can alter the frequency of our being. The frequency of energy in physical reality was quite dense, slow moving and restricted. As we attune ourselves to more Spiritual realms of consciousness, our vibrations can become lighter, finer and more loving. For us to be able to connect with our Spiritual guides, the frequency of vibration of our being and theirs need to match up and to be compatible. So, there is a mutual process of adjustment needed whereby the guide needs to lower their vibration from its usual state, and we need to raise ours so that then communication can be achieved.

Once a connection with our guide is made consciously, it will be easier to achieve that again. The contact becomes stronger and develops as we practice attuning to our guides in our meditation.

Usually our Spiritual guides will present a name for themselves to us, if we can pick this up. This gives us a reference to make it easier for us to connect with them. In our meditation, then, we can repeat the name of our guide like a mantra, and this will help bring the presence of our guide very close to us.

People needed to go step by step in opening their awareness to other realities and contacting guides. Some people can go into these deeper states of consciousness far easier than others. Temperamentally, some people quite naturally take refuge in their inner realities and feel safe there, perhaps more safe than facing the rigours and demands of the physical world. The receptive instinctive side of these people's nature can be much more strongly developed than the analytical side, and therefore, they are inclined to relish their psychic sensitivity, but they might not be very grounded. Other people feel safest in keeping a firm hold upon the physical world and confining their attention to this reality so they can manage it and direct it. The fears of letting go of control will be much greater for these people but progress is still be possible if it is something that the person wishes. Ideally we need to find a balance between these two sides of our nature

The process of learning to open our inner awareness can be quite delicate. Sometimes, we would have people coming to our healing group that became frustrated. When they tried meditation, they would feel that they could not leave their bodies, they could not go on any interesting inner journeys, and they might not even be able to let go of everyday thoughts and relax. When their expectations could not be met, they would be ready to give up.

Sojah often told us that our Spiritual guides were much closer to us than we realized. He gave an analogy where he suggested that it was like our guides were in a room immediately adjacent to us. All we had to do was to open the door between and we could be with them. It was helpful if we could believe in our capacity to make contact, and then we needed to give time and space for this to happen.

Very often, the process of opening our inner awareness is a gradual process where much patience and perseverance is needed. I remember in our healing group that there would be members of our group that would gently strive for months and months to try to make a direct contact with their Spiritual guides, and feel that very little was happening as evidence that they were making progress. Then one evening, there could be a change. The appearance of the guide or an inner journey out of the body could take place very suddenly when it is ready to occur. But all those months of waiting would not have been wasted. In all probability, much inner preparation and building of inner links would have been taking place during this time that would have been quite invisible to our surface consciousness.

Not everyone finds it possible to detach themselves completely from their physical body through meditation. But it can still be possible to be in contact with our Spiritual guide, whether or not we can achieve this. Thought and energy transfer with our guide can take place in many circumstances and sometimes quite unexpectedly, during the course of our everyday life. Our guides have various means by which they can try to communicate with us. The most usual means is by telepathy, but they can also use inner symbols, or feelings that we will sense, or even by influences in our dreams.

In my own experience, it has usually been through thought that I have sensed the presence of my guide. Thought impressions have come into my mind that just appear a little bit different to my own. They have manifested with a feeling of peace, assuredness and quietness that I have come to recognize as belonging to my guide. Sometimes, these thoughts pass into and out of my mind very quickly, and if my mind is occupied with other things, I can miss what my guide wants to convey to me. I can imagine with my own awareness that I only pick up a small percentage of guidance that is given to me, because I do not take sufficient notice of it in the moments it is given to me. This is where we need to train ourselves to become inwardly alert and ready to accept help from our Spiritual sources. As we become mindful of the thoughts we carry in our everyday life, we will choose positive thoughts, and not fill our minds with preoccupations that would preclude our guide from communicating with us.

Our minds can regulate hugely what we find acceptable as a notion or idea and what we would rather ignore. By choosing a Spiritual path, we engage in practices like meditation so that we can open our minds to what is true within, and gradually let go to our attachments of habits and how we feel our life has to be. Once we engage in a Spiritual path, our life will, in all likelihood, become much more fluid and feel inwardly free rather than being stuck in fixed patterns where our sense of aliveness is more limited.

Prayer is further avenue for us to develop our inner awareness. We can direct our prayers outwards as an effort to wish to help others, but we can also ask 'God', our guides, or our inner wisdom, to help us in areas of our life of our own inner development where we feel we need help. As we put requests and inner wishes to our sources within us, our inner consciousness will naturally act and adjust to try to meet the needs that we have expressed. Whatever preoccupies us; our inner mind will adjust to that and form itself around these concerns. Our state of mind is determined so much by our thought choices and what we direct inwardly, more so than outer circumstances. By taking responsibility for our choices of thought, our outer circumstances might also begin to change, and opportunities could come to us that we had not anticipated.

Sojah emphasized, on many occasions, his concept, that life on all levels, including the various Spiritual planes, is involved in a learning and unfolding process, that somehow we are all learning together, and that this is also the case in terms of our making contact with our guides. It is as much for our guides to learn how they can connect with us as it is for us with them. On all levels of life, choices can be made that will affect our destiny and those around us. Nothing is set, and even plans that are made on very high Spiritual levels, can be affected by choices made by the individual wills of those concerned.

Once we start to dedicate ourselves to a Spiritual path, we feel more peace and acceptance inwardly. There is a growing sense of connection and fellowship of love with all around us, something that we can nurture and allow to grow. We might have our trials and challenges, and the outer circumstances of our lives may appear very difficult, but it is what we feel within that matters, and that is where our faith can flourish. Our learning takes place one step at a time, and meditation, prayer and contemplation as well as practicing kindness in our everyday life can help us on this journey.

# Part 2 – Chapter 6

## Healing ourselves, healing others

What I valued most in our healing group was the care and love that was present. It was towards healing that our attention was directed, and healing is an act of offering help to others. When we met together, we would send healing to others outside our Circle through Absent Healing. Then we would offer healing to each other through Spiritual Healing. At the end of our healing evenings, we would ask for the Spiritual energies that we had gathered, to spread out from the room where we were, to go to people and places where it was needed. Members of the group gained a deep sense of fulfillment engaging in these activities. There was something about channeling love and healing that felt sacred and wonderfully precious.

Sojah made clear that with regards his work of teaching, helping people to develop and work through their problems, and gain Spiritual awareness, that as a consequence of doing these things, he would be able to move higher in the planes in his own development too. People in our group were interested to develop their own Spiritual gifts. However, the main essence of our activities was always to help others, to love and care, and channel Spiritual love to our Earth, and serve humanity. What we gained for ourselves was linked to that, because we all do need to honour our own needs, but was secondary.

When we on Earth choose a path of love and service to others, this helps us to connect to Spirit and our true nature. Such a path cannot be forced. We need to feel in our hearts that this is what we truly want to do before any efforts we make in this direction will be effective.

Not every soul has a plan where loving others is an important ingredient. As examples, a soul might choose a lifetime where they want to concentrate on survival in tough circumstances, or where they need to apply themselves to some achievement that does not have much to do with others, or even where they need to focus upon working out their relationship with one other soul. These kinds of soul experiences can provide important learning too.

But where people feel in their hearts and souls, that they want to care, and help and serve others with love, doing this can bring much joy and happiness. This is what Sojah meant by bringing the Spiritual and physical worlds together. As we dedicate ourselves to being true to our hearts, to caring and helping others, then this enables us to more fully be in harmony with Spirit, and we can raise our energy vibrations by virtue of the resonance that is there in our activities along with Spirit.

There might come a time in a person's life where it is the right time for him or her, as a soul, to engage in healing and service towards others. Before then, there might be many experiences that the person needs to encounter so that they will be ready. Very often, that person may need to undergo their own healing journey in order to prepare them to be able to be of service. As we learn about what needs healing within ourselves, and then undergo that process, it prepares us and opens the compassion in our heart to be able to help others. Learning to love is a step-by-step process, like placing stones together to construct a building.

Sojah often expressed sadness with his observation of how so many people in our world did not care, and were wrapped up in their wants and needs, with little awareness or concern for anyone else. When people were like this, their auras were dull and unresponsive. Where love was lacking, the connection that they shared with others would be more about habit, conditions and attachment. Life then, could feel hard, empty and painful. Sojah observed that there were many people whose inner path might be one where they could gain much fulfillment by caring and offering loving service to others, but while they did not recognize that, they would feel emptiness and little that they did would give any true feelings of satisfaction.

When people got caught up with difficult feelings such as fear, guilt, shame, resentment, anger or despair, then the thoughts associated with these feelings would affect the aura. The love and vibrancy that would naturally flow through us from Spirit would be restricted and distorted by the manifestation of these feelings, especially when they became more entrenched. Our aura might not then function very well, and could be termed as being sick or ill.

Once the energy system of our body is weakened and less radiant than it could be, then this can have an impact on the physical body. For our physical body to be nourished spiritually, we need for the energy system of our body to be flowing freely. In places where this is not happening, then this can have an impact upon the physical health of our body.

For instance, if we feel rejected by somebody, we might feel that as a pain in our heart, and the energy system of our body may be restricted in the extent that it can flow around our heart centre. This in turn could make it more difficult for our physical heart to do the work that it needs to do because it is lacking Spiritual energy, so the prospect of illness connected with our heart and all the organs associated with it, will be increased.

There might be important learning for us to gain from working through these difficult feelings, and once our aura is less radiant, then we will naturally turn inwards with our attention and be more occupied with our own inner state. What we do about that will be up to us. If we seek understanding, then our challenging times can be springboards for us to gain inner resolution and move forward on our path. When we recover and we are in a state where our energy system is flowing, then we might be in a position where we can better help others through similar difficulties.

Not all illness has its roots in prior difficulties that exist in the energetic system. Some illnesses do have physical causes, and their occurrence will have a dampening affect upon the aura, whatever thoughts and feelings are going on for us. However, if the aura is adversely affected by emotional and mental disturbances, that may be at a sub-conscious level, then the onset of, say, a virus, like the common cold, is likely to have a much more severe impact on that body, than with someone whose aura was typically in balance and flowing with vitality.

People have a responsibility to care for their own physical, energetic and Spiritual being. Through our thoughts, feelings and physical actions, we influence our health and well-being. Our thoughts, feelings and actions are generated by our free will and so we choose what we express and how we do it. Whatever we are told by others, or conditioned to think, we all need to believe that we are worthy of love, not only giving it out to others, but allowing it for ourselves as well. We are created out of love, so for us to embrace that love is for us to be in harmony with our essence.

With all the various events in our life, it is up to us how we react to those. If we are confronted by something violent or traumatic that happens to us, we still need to make an effort to try to come to terms with that if we can. We can easily carry emotional residues of hatred, anger, sadness, despair or shame, for instance, when an event takes place that feels more than we can cope with. Sometimes these disturbing emotions can be projected towards other people, 'God', or the event itself. But if we lock these feelings away inside us, the only person that these emotions will ultimately be damaging will be our Self. Sooner or later, we will have to clear these disturbances if we want our aura to be vibrant and in balance, and if we wish to be in harmony with our greater soul. It is normal though, to carry some unwanted feelings inside us. As children, especially, we are not equipped to withstand all the influences to which we are exposed. As humans, we do make mistakes.

By the way we deal with the various situations in our life, we will build up patterns of reactions in our sub-conscious minds. Our instincts will be moulded by what we expect to be true, and the way we respond to circumstances is unlikely to be wise all the time. Therefore, there will be belief systems that we have constructed, existing in our sub-conscious minds, which regulate how we behave. Some of these modes of behaviour might not be in tune with the needs of our soul, and it will be a challenge for us to address this.

When we engage in regular meditation, we might find that there are periods where we don't seem to go so deep, and there are disquieting thoughts and feelings that arise. This might be because there are disturbing beliefs and experiences that we have carried in our sub-conscious minds that need to come to the surface and be released. When we meditate, our guides and Higher self, can work with us to cleanse and clear our consciousness of unwanted residues. Because we are quiet and receptive in meditation, we can be more easily in harmony with the Spiritual aspect of our nature. Although the process of cleansing our limiting inner energy patterns can feel uncomfortable, when we have completed a clearing, we will feel better.

With meditation and contemplation, where we feel troubled in our thoughts, feelings and perhaps even our physical health, we can seek understanding from deep within us for these, and ask for Spiritual help. Once we gain understanding of the root of a problem, then it will cease to be a disturbance beyond our control. We will be able then to choose, whether we wish to continue that limiting pattern or not.

Sometimes, there can be a lot for us to work out. There can be destructive thoughts and feelings that have accumulated and meshed together in our energy system. There is only so much that we can carry in our normal consciousness. Consequently, many of these problems may then be etched in our inner sub-consciousness, but will still affect our energy system and could be creating disturbances without us being consciously aware of what is happening.

It is part of our journey as souls, to manage those thoughts and feelings that we carry and to work with them, so that hopefully we eventually can bring love and transformation to all the dark places in our being. But we can only take one step at a time, and learn what we are able to learn with our awareness, before we can move forward.

Miracles can occur. If a person has been suffering in some form, and they have been working inwardly to seek guidance and help sufficiently, then it might happen, when the conditions and the timing according to that soul's need are right, that some dramatic transformation and change can manifest for that person. Miracles are like an act of Grace, and can seem like good fortune coming into that person's life. When they occur, it is appropriate to give thanks to miracles as a blessing, so that what has occurred can be fully honoured and appreciated. On an inner soul level though, this occurrence will have been arranged, and probably earned as a reward for some inner achievement.

I have shared in my book, 'Healing Journeys' of a miracle that Marjorie experienced, when I first started healing with her. She had an ugly module on her hand. It was the size of a golf ball, and her consultant had decided that it needed an operation to remove it. Within a few months of healing, this module had completely disappeared.

Spirit is often working behind the scenes to help us. Sometimes there can be a series of seemingly unrelated events that gradually build up in our lives, and then one day, we can reflect and realize how all that we have been experiencing has a meaning and underlying purpose that we had not sensed previously. We might have a dream, or an energy release in a healing session. We could be walking in the street, or in a psychotherapy session. Moments of inner realization can occur, and when they do, can bring with them, great feelings of peace, or release, sometimes feeling like a great burden has gone.

There are times when we have to face a trial in our lives and make decisions relating to that, before we can receive any obvious help. As souls, we need to feel that we can stand on our own feet, and test our strength and abilities. It is often the case that we will only realize what we have done after we have been through an experience. But as we feel that 'God', or Spirit is walking with us, it will give us a lot more confidence to proceed, and trust the impulses that we feel we must express.

We can carry so many negative scripts within our minds. There can be thoughts that we are useless, hopeless, stupid, and ugly, that nobody will love us or care for us, that we are incapable of getting it right. All of these types of thoughts will act as a block preventing us from receiving love. They might feel like a wall and barrier that we put around us, or a knot that we carry. There might be a part of us that feels empty and has given up.

It must be emphasized again that these are conditions that we create ourselves. The reality is that we are 'children of God', and our essence is love, so these scripts are illusions that keep us from expressing our true nature. It is a necessary component of the human condition that we have to work through these. But if we can trace deep into the root of these encumbrances, and be mindful of the essential love that is our being, then we will be able to let these go, and advance our learning in the process.

Sojah often remarked to us about the value of laughter. Life can have so many layers of complexity and various perspectives, and be at the same time, simple and still. With all the seeming contradictions, our perception can experience many surprises and radical shifts in our awareness. All of this can be very funny. Laughter is an appreciation of the joy and wonder of life. If we get caught up in one particular viewpoint of a situation, then laughter can help dispel this so we can embrace more wholeness. With laughter comes acceptance and joy, and it is very comforting. It is a quality that exists on the Spiritual planes as much as the physical. In our healing group, we sometimes experienced this, and it brought a great deal of happiness to us all.

One means of help that we can receive directly from Spirit is the gift of Spiritual Healing. What this entails is the transference of Spiritual love and specific healing energies into our aura, so that this can work upon disturbances and distortions that are limiting us and help these to be removed or altered for the energy to flow freely. Ultimately, as I have described, all healing is self-healing, because healing will only take place when we open to it, and inwardly consent to it, and when we feel that we are ready to receive it. People can place their hands upon us and ask to channel healing to us, and we can also receive Spiritual help through others' prayers and distant healing. It will only have a deep impact though, when we are open within us for help, and willing to change.

In our healing group, it was Dagmar, my Healing guide, who addressed us through Marjorie, issues related to Spiritual healing. It appeared that in Spirit, beings could study and learn to specialize in various areas of expression and gain expertise. In healing, it was Dagmar who was given the right to speak, while with Spiritual teachings, it was Sojah that was given deference over others, and he always addressed his teachings and imparted them with great dignity.

Dagmar spoke with great enthusiasm about healing, encouraging us to open our hearts and try it with people that needed help. We only had to ask, and Spirit was there waiting and ready to intercede on our behalf.

When we care and love others, we can also transmit healing to them. We all need love to survive and to flourish. To channel Spiritual healing, we need to ask Spirit to work through us, so it is not our energy reaching the person that needs help, but energy given to us from Spirit, that flows through us. As we ask for help from Spirit, then Spirit will do its best to respond. We have to trust that when we channel healing, and open our faith, energy will reach where it is needed.

With Spiritual healing, there will be the healing channel, the person receiving healing, and Spirit. The healing channel will open themselves to care for the person in need, will ask permission from the soul of the person receiving to do healing work, and then ask Spirit through prayer and invocation, to be a healing channel so that healing can be drawn into the person that has asked for it. The person receiving can best facilitate the healing process by closing eyes, inwardly inviting the healing to take place, and then being open for the experience to take place. By virtue of the invitation that has been given, Spirit can then do its work on the energy field of the person receiving healing.

The process of healing takes place on a subtler realm of consciousness than the physical, but its effects can be felt physically.

Once I remember, I was channeling healing to a man who was wearing thick Hobnail boots. I placed my hands on his boots. To me, while I was doing that, the feeling in my hands felt quite normal and I had to trust in Spirit that something worthwhile was being channeled for my patient. Afterwards though, the man told me that he had felt intense heat coming from my hands through his boots and penetrating deep into his feet. It is clear that this heat was not physical in nature because, certainly, his boots felt no different in temperature. Also, as a manifestation of energy, it went beyond my usual conscious awareness, because I did not realize what was happening. The effect of receiving this heat energy enabled my patient to feel much calmer and more grounded, something that benefited him. It was experiences such as these that made it very easy for members of our healing group to build up a strong faith and belief in the reality of Spirit.

According to Sojah and Dagmar, Spiritual beings that specialize in healing can come close when healing energies are invoked. The source of healing is 'God', that essential love energy at the heart of all creation. Quantities of this energy can be harnessed by these Spiritual beings. They can direct it in specific ways for particular purposes. This energy can be grounded in the physical plane through the Healer by his/her faith and openness, and also the caring and love in his/her heart. The more attuned the healer can be to the Spiritual beings that are there; the better those healing energies can flow.

While on one of her inner Spiritual journeys, Marjorie once had a vision of the healing energy that healers in the Spiritual realm, such as Dagmar, could tap into. It was like a vast, never ending stream of energy, full of colour, vibrancy and love. The power of it was immense. Marjorie was in awe of it when she experienced it.

Spiritual beings specializing in healing can be very skilled at manipulating energy. Some of them can do Spiritual operations and repair damage to people's energy system in correspondence with work on the physical plane that could be done by surgeons. As repairs are performed on an energetic level, this can filter through to help the physical being too.

There are limits though, to what can be achieved through healing from Spirit. Healing transformation can take place only if the soul concerned is in a position to receive that healing and also if it is that soul's choice for the healing to occur. Sometimes, quite a number of arrangements need to be in place from both the Spiritual and physical side, before healing can happen.

There could be the soul plan in place for two souls to meet on Earth when both have reached a particular stage in their development, and for healing then to be given and received, either for reasons of potential Spiritual growth for both, or as a resolution of some karmic issue that was incomplete. Likewise, a soul may have chosen a form of death or illness as part of their path, again, either for possible learning or to clear imbalances from the past. Here, healing may not be able to prevent that illness or death taking place, but could help bring peace so the experience can be accepted more easily, provided the person is open to receive.

Our human will can also interfere and limit the effectiveness of healing. For instance, somebody may be suffering with depression, and open him or herself for a healing session. After the healing, they could feel great, and their energy system cleared of negativity. However, if that person has habits and limiting thought patterns that are linked to living conditions that they don't like, then as they slip back into these, the difficult conditions of the depression will return.

Sometimes, people may want very much to be healed, and yet, spiritual healing does not help them. There could be aspects of our self beneath the surface of the everyday consciousness that block the healing. These parts of our self can be in conflict with what we want with our external self, and so for us to learn what they need can enable us to become more integrated. It could be an aspect of our child consciousness, or a part of us that feels very lost and confused. This part of us may not feel that it deserves healing or believe that nothing can help. If we can identify and then listen to what these fragments of our being need, we can begin a process of healing. We might have to overcome our own negative judgment of these parts first. Very often, what they will need most is love and acceptance. As we give this to them we will be engaging in another step of learning to love our self more fully. In these cases, healing can bring up an awareness of these conditions and provide an opportunity for us to learn something important from deep inside. We may need help with this, either with someone who is sensitive to this kind of work, or with our Spiritual guide, if we feel a close trusting connection there. Through acknowledgement and acceptance, we can release blockages that these fragments were carrying and live in a state of greater inner freedom and harmony with our essential self. We need to listen to our intuition and instinct to determine if blockages like this exist within us. Then, if they do, prayer, meditation and perhaps psychotherapy can help us investigate what is needed to work them out.

In our everyday life, the people we meet and the situations that we encounter do not occur by accident. They all exist as opportunities for us to learn, and if we are on a Spiritual path, for us to serve and help in some way. All of life exists as a reflection of 'God' and 'God's love', and as we open to that, we can also feel the joy in our hearts that is 'God' and then express a little more of that love, which is our core being. By doing this, we will grow in the ways of Spirit. We will be able to embrace more of what is without and within ourselves. Healing will be the peace and love of feeling our connectedness with life around us, and the joy of expressing our individual path, as part of this.

# Part 2 – Chapter 7
# Challenges in our modern society

Sojah taught us about the value of love and acceptance. Living life on our Earth is full of potential trials and challenges. Spirit is here to help us, and we only need to reach out for it, and Spirit will try to support us. Our guides and Spiritual helpers cannot necessarily change a situation with which we are involved, but can help us to understand, find peace and insight, so that we can deal with the situation and learn from it in the best possible manner. Through meditation, contemplation and prayer, we can gain guidance to enable us to move forward on our Spiritual path.

It was of concern to Sojah that when we did not have Spirit at the heart of our life, that our actions could easily become destructive. We could get wrapped up in states of mind such as greed, selfish indulgences, hate, aggression, prejudice and fear. When these drives and emotions became predominant, then this would have a negative impact on the world around us. Sojah felt that many of the trends in our contemporary society, made it more difficult for people to relax, to love and feel close to Spirit. When people became obsessed with money, for instance, with little regard for others, this would put up barriers between people. The rush and bustle of city life did not promote happiness or the space for people to tune into their deeper inner needs.

Sojah felt that unless there was a greater awareness of Spirit in our civilization as a whole, that eventually humanity could destroy our Earth. We would be the ones responsible for that. It is chilling to realize that we could do that to ourselves. This outcome is not inevitable but is possible.

It was suggested that many efforts are being made on the Spiritual side to try to help our humanity and allow conditions to be established that would be conducive for our life on Earth to improve. Souls come to Earth with great plans of how they can put things right, but those plans are not always fulfilled in the manner intended. With our free will, we can easily become distracted from our soul intentions, and where others are involved, they can also be diverted from fulfilling their purpose, so where co-operation is needed, this may not be achieved.

Sojah did prophesize that at some point in the twenty first century, there would be a very highly evolved Spiritual being coming into physical incarnation with the aim of helping our humanity and that this could make a significant difference to us.

The veil between our physical existence and Spiritual reality is lessening at the moment. This implies that people can more easily gain direct experience of Spirit and open to Spiritual impulses in their lives. As people reach out for this, more Spiritual energies will be released and barriers between our reality and the Spiritual realm will be diminished further.

When people meet together in groups or as individuals and channel Spirit onto the Earth for healing or personal awareness, then this spiritually lights up the energy field around these people and draws Spirit closer. As these groups and individuals link up with each other, through common purpose, the light of Spirit has more focus points and builds up like a fabric across the globe. When enough of these light centres are established, and they have sufficient strength, then this could transform the consciousness of our humanity on Earth. This was the hope that Sojah expressed – this is something towards which people that cared for our humanity could work.

However, there are many people and places on the Earth where the light of Spirit cannot easily penetrate, areas of darkness where people's hearts are not open and conditions are worsening. It is a struggle.

There were then questions of what we can do in our everyday life to make a difference. Is there a right way of doing things?

Sojah was often asked if there were any special Spiritual practices that people needed to do, any diet that would be better, or if people were doing healing, whether there was some approach to doing healing that would be more powerful and effective? In response to this, Sojah counselled that people needed to do what they believed was right. There was generally no absolutely right way or wrong way of doing things. People needed to be true to their own inner guidance and live according to that. We also needed to respect that everyone has their own path and we are each responsible for the decisions that we make. What was most important was for people to have open hearts.

With religion, although Sojah agreed that while some doctrines in various religions could be limiting and even prejudicial, these doctrines more came from people's interpretation of Spiritual truth rather than the Spiritual experience that inspired the teachings in the first place. We needed to be tolerant of each other, and our various beliefs. Faith in 'God' and worship could be very important as a means to bring Spirit closer to the person concerned, and would bring with it, a lot of peace.

On the subjects of technology and science, Sojah could acknowledge the advancements that these have made to our living conditions. For example, through technology, we are able to communicate with people around the world. This enables us to have a sense of connectedness with all other people on the planet. Through medical research, people can live healthier and longer lives. However, it could also be argued with, say, our transport system, that while it helps us to move locations, it also contributes to raising stress and creating pollution. Having developed planes that can fly has resulted in fighter planes that can cause huge amounts of destruction.

Sojah tended to have quite a neutral attitude towards these scientific expressions of our humanity. From a Spiritual perspective, the important issue is not so much about how clever we can be, and how well we can manipulate the environment, but more about how much love we can generate and channel to enable people to find true fulfillment.

Sometimes Sojah would suggest lifestyles from our past did have some virtues, and that a simple life where people are connected to the Earth and are able to enjoy the peace of trees and animals could be more conducive to happiness and a spiritual outlook to life, than the fast paced complicated society of today.

In our present environment, there are many pressures. We live in a consumer society, where we are encouraged to buy more than we need. In the business world, there is competition, exploitation and the need to be effective with resources. People often work long hours, and are required to perform duties that often feel alien to them. In our cities, there is so much concrete, noise and chaotic activity, that it is not very conducive for people to find peace.

Many people take drugs as a means of escaping from the world, and inducing feelings that they could not find otherwise. Sadly, these drugs do not build the love of our soul and can be very destructive to our energy system. It is an indication of the thirst that so many have for spiritual experience and fulfillment that drug taking is so prevalent.

In the wider world, natural habitats are being destroyed, wars and terrorism are creating pain and suffering, overcrowded conditions are bringing about widespread hunger and famine to millions. It seems that when we look at our world, there is a lot that could be better.

It might be our destiny to help others, and perhaps to work with others to make some difference in our world. We cannot force people to change. If we feel the urge to do something to help, we need to listen within for what that may be and how we can best do it. There could be people we can meet to help us. It is worth trying.

With our healing group, it was on a Spiritual level that we tried to be of service, spreading out love, connecting inwardly with other light centres around the globe.

There is much to be done on many levels, but first we need to be at peace with ourselves. Otherwise, what we attempt is likely to be futile.

In terms of our individual life, Sojah counselled that, where possible, it would be beneficial for us to spend quiet times, doing what we love doing. When we are faced with trials and challenges, if we ask for help from others, and listen inside for guidance, we could move forward one step at a time. In those moments when we are in the midst of difficulties, it is usually helpful to be patient, and seek understanding for what is confronting us rather than trying to struggle against it. We needed to trust that what needed to come forward for us in our lives would do so, and encourage that by keeping an open and positive mind. As human beings, we need to be kind to ourselves. As we open to Spirit, we will feel that sense of well-being that we do have a place in the greater scheme of things, and there will be the urge in us to live our part in that and contribute what we can.

# *Part 3 – Sojah's meditations*

At the end of our Healing group evenings, Sojah would lead us into a meditation. These meditations were very relaxing, but they were also intended by Sojah to be part of our Spiritual training. Each one was unique, but many of the meditations would be variations on similar themes. Sojah's intention was to help us open our psychic and Spiritual faculties and to more easily connect with our Spiritual guides. He also wished for us to learn to be able to detach ourselves from our physical body, so that through meditation we could rise up out of our bodies with our awareness and experience the love and wonders of the Spiritual realms, and especially the Summerland, directly. Sojah would sometimes describe elements of the Summerland to us to help us tune into it. He wanted us to be reassured that we could welcome these experiences and that we would be safe and inwardly protected. All we needed to do was to call on our guides to be present and they would be there for us.

Many of Sojah's meditations were recorded on tape and transcribed. In this chapter, I am including adaptations of four of his meditations. It is planned that these will be available on CD so those interested can use them.

**Third eye meditation**

When Sojah talked to us of meditation, he often described how when we could release the cares and restrictions of our personality self, then our consciousness could rise up, like a submarine with its periscope. When it reached high enough, we could perceive what it was like in Spirit. We could train ourselves and develop skills to be able to do this. He suggested that the more we could learn about Spirit while in our physical bodies, the easier it would be for us when we passed over. One of the main ways that Sojah taught us to approach meditation was through working with our third eye, the psychic centre in the middle of our forehead.

He told us that we could imagine as if we had an actual eye there. Then, when we closed our physical eyes, we could gaze with our third eye, into the darkness of our inner mind, and just be open to what we could perceive there. If we were patient and persevered with this, then sooner or later, visions and other experiences could reveal themselves. It is a means for us to open our psychic awareness.

Most of Sojah's meditations were orientated towards helping us to raise our consciousness out of our physical body to experience Spirit directly. However, the following is a simple meditation he introduced to us, that is designed to encourage the practice of working Spiritually with the third eye. It uses a counting method from ten backwards towards one as part of the preparation, as a means to deepen our inner concentration. Here it is:

*For this meditation, make yourself comfortable, sitting or lying, as you prefer. Be in a room or setting that is quiet and where you are not likely to be disturbed. Then you can start by closing your eyes and focusing upon your breathing. Just breathe steadily and allow the rhythm of your breathing to settle as you relax and go within yourself.*

*As well as providing a means for you to practice using the third eye this meditation is also intended to help you establish a clearer connection with your Spiritual guides.*

*So, find yourself now beginning to relax, your body getting heavier and feeling very comfortably relaxed, feeling that relaxation extend right through your body, so you can just let go, and enjoy. Feel with your awareness that you are reaching upwards, becoming lighter, even though you stay connected with your physical body.*

*Now, concentrate your attention upon the centre of your forehead. Allow visions, thoughts, and sensations to be there. You may perceive sparks of light or energy. It could be very quiet and dark. Observe and be still. Let the experience unfold.*

*As you continue to focus upon your third eye, count very slowly from ten to one. With each number, your inner awareness grows stronger and clearer... Ten...nine...eight...seven...six...five...four...three...two...and one...You are now very deeply relaxed, and your inner eye is open. Let yourself gaze with your third eye. Welcome any visions that are there. Listen to the thoughts that come into your mind. Sense with your instinct what is happening. Whatever comes to you, be open and honour your perception. Your third eye is opening. You are able to do this better and better.*

*(Long pause)*

*You call on your Spiritual guide now, and their presence comes close to you. You open your awareness to the love and peaceful energy of your guide. More and more, you are learning to distinguish their reassuring being. They are here to help you, and you recognize them with you. They may be in front of you or above, or by your side. You sense where they are and what they want to share with you. With your third eye, you might see your guide in the form that they appear to you. Let this awareness grow, inside your mind. Even if it is only dim, just be with it now and let it unfold. It could be a light, a shining light. Whatever comes to you, just continue to be with it, so that it can begin to take shape and form. You can do this.*

*It might be possible for you to converse with your guide. You sense what your guide wants to impart to you, and you listen, and if you have a question, you ask it. Your ability to do this grows with practice, and you are becoming more Spiritually sensitive. There could be a vision or symbol that your guide wants to show you, to help you on your path.*

*Take some time to continue this, now, in silence.*

(Long Pause)

*This meditation is a resource that you can practice every day. It can help to develop your inner awareness and provide an opportunity for you to receive Spiritual guidance. For now, we are going to conclude this for today.*

*Taking in every thing you have experienced, slowly and gradually, let yourself return slowly to your normal state of consciousness. Your third eye also adjusts so it can function once more at a rate that supports you in your everyday life. Feel yourself again in your physical body and able to move. Let this take place at a rate that is right for you. And finally, only when you are ready, and feel your consciousness in your physical body, open your eyes.*

**The light at the end of the tunnel meditation**

Sometimes in their meditations, members of our healing group would find themselves going on an inner journey through a tunnel. Sojah explained that travelling though a tunnel could be a route to link with Spirit. When we found the light at the end of the tunnel, then this light could be actually a direct experience of Spirit, and that when we reached this place, we could then meet with the presence of loved ones that had passed on, and also our Spiritual guides and helpers. As we adjusted to the Spiritual light, we could also then be aware of details of what the Spiritual realm was like.

Sojah referred to Marjorie, and that in her earlier years, in her dreams and at moments when she was resting with her eyes closed, she would sometimes experience a tunnel, and that there was somebody at the end of it, waiting to help. It was her soul journey to realize that Sojah was the one at the end of the tunnel, and that she had now reached the point where she knew this.

This meditation is one where the light at the end of the tunnel is deliberately invoked as a Spiritual exercise. Here it follows:

*To begin this meditation, find yourself a quiet and relaxing place where you are not likely to be disturbed. Choose to either sit comfortably or lie down, and then lets prepare to start.*

*Close your eyes, and focus on your breathing. Allow your breathing to adjust and find a gentle regular rhythm. Do that very easily. Just imagine that your body is becoming heavier and heavier, so heavy that you don't feel that you can move. But in this state, you feel quite comfortable and becoming free. Your awareness is becoming more and more still and calm.*

*Then you can focus steadily upon the centre of your forehead, because that is where your third eye is situated. Very slowly, just sense that you are opening this inner eye, like you would if you were opening a curtain. Let this happen so that you feel that it is open. With this eye, you can see so much more, because this is the psychic part of you.*

*As you begin to see with your psychic eye, imagine that very slightly, you are beginning to rock and sway. The heaviness of your body is slipping away and you feel lightness is coming to you. You perceive the light permeating through you. This lightness increases your sense of inner freedom, and then slowly, you feel yourself rising upwards. With your awareness, you are rising up, up, up, and with each motion upwards, you feel more and more free. You welcome this feeling. Then, a little to your left, there is a tunnel.*

*If you do not see the tunnel, just sense it, as if it is there. This tunnel is beckoning you. You feel drawn to it, and find that you are drifting towards this. You know you can enter this tunnel if you wish, so you make a choice. I will continue now, as if your decision is to proceed.*

*Now, you travel into this tunnel. As you enter, there is a feeling of warmth. In this tunnel with you are other loving Spiritual beings. You may or may not see them, but they are there to help you, and their presence is reassuring. If for any reason, you feel nervous or hesitate, you can ask softly for inner help, and there will be guiding hands to assist you. You can accept this and let it unfold. There is love around you, and you feel like you are moving on. In the distance, you sense the end of the tunnel, and you are coming closer to that. And what you sense at the end of the tunnel is light.*

*Now, go towards this light. Concentrate on this light, and as you get nearer, the light, of course, gets bigger and bigger, till you realize that you are at the end of the tunnel. And now, if you wish, you can step forward and out of the tunnel. Just do that now, and you find that you are in the light. It is wonderful.*

*There is a presence with you, a very beautiful and loving presence, and this is your guide, who has been waiting for you. With your guide, you feel accepted to be just who you are. There is a deep feeling of peace. You feel very close to them and are able to speak with your mind. Your guide is ready to take you on a Spiritual journey and you welcome this.*

*In the Spiritual realm, there is much beauty and love. It is like home for you because you came from Spirit before you were born. You adjust your perception and begin to sense details of the place where you are. Your guide becomes clearer to you and takes on a form so that you can recognize his or her appearance. You sense the brilliant energy of your guide as distinct from your own, and you welcome him or her as a very dear friend who knows you intimately and can help you with love.*

*You become aware of the scenery around you. There may be mountains, trees, water or buildings. However the environment appears to you, you feel safe and at ease and your senses are filled with a radiance of light.*

*In the Spirit realm, there are special Halls where you can visit. There is the Hall of Love. For those who have been suffering from loneliness or going through difficulties on their own, this Hall can bring forward love energies to replenish you and enable you to feel much happiness. Another place is the Halls of Healing. Here, if your energy system is out of alignment, there are Healers on hand to help you and soothe your problems with wonderful Spiritual energies. There are Halls of Learning where you can study and gain Spiritual knowledge about the nature of reality. Other Halls include the Halls of Music, where it is possible, through thought, to create and generate beautiful sounds, or else appreciate someone else that is expressing those. Beside the Halls, there are so many places of interest for you to experience, and where you can grow and learn.*

*Now with your guide, you go on your own journey. Just experience it, and enjoy. With your guide, you can communicate by sharing thoughts together. Trust your instincts and with your awareness and your guide's help, you will know what to do. Take some moments to explore this.*

*(Long pause)*

*Sadly now, you need to leave. You can bring back with you the memory, and cherish this. The experience you have had has been a time of happiness and sharing, and you can repeat this meditation to go on further journeys with your guide, on other occasions.*

*Slowly now, imagine that you are connecting again with your physical body, feeling that you are gently sliding back into your physical body, so that you can feel your limbs and know that you have returned. There could be a moment when it feels heavy and not quite comfortable, as you adjust. You know that you have a life in the physical body that you need to live now and this experience that you have had of Spirit can help you, because of the love you have felt. Gradually then, only when you feel fully in your body, you can open your eyes, with a feeling of well being, remembering everything you have experienced.*

### Cleansing meditation

One day, when I was working with her, Marjorie was taken on an inner Spiritual journey to a room. In this room, there were objects that she could smash. It was a time when Marjorie had been feeling very angry and frustrated at both her inability to do what she wanted, and the dependency she felt upon others. Being in this room, she could express those feelings and release the tension that had been gathered inside her. It provided a space for her to act potently and without the danger that she could hurt someone else in the process. With Marjorie's abilities, even though the experience was on an energetic level, it felt very real to her. She felt the presence of Sojah afterwards, and they talked together. When she returned to her normal consciousness, Marjorie felt much more calm and peaceful, and connected with Spirit. The peace she felt was sustained for many days following on from this.

Like Marjorie, we all have times when frustrations and difficulties build up inside us. It is not always easy to find a constructive outlet for these feelings. When engaged on a Spiritual path, it is natural to wish to care for others and to help them. It can be quite awkward if we feel bogged down by our own emotional state, and not as giving and loving, as we would like to be. The challenge for us can be about how we can best deal with our inner difficulties without projecting them onto others and affecting those with whom we are in contact, negatively.

It may be our wish to be very kind and loving in all our actions, but as humans, that is not really possible. People who strive to give and be helpful, are not always so capable of opening up to receive help themselves when they need it. Yet, this balance is essential to maintain for us to keep our own channels open, and for us to feel connected with those that we are striving to help.

One evening in our Healing group, the energy in the room was very sluggish. Although there was the usual willingness to go through all the stages of ritual as we normally did, there was not that spark of inspiration that we were accustomed to feeling together. It transpired that many members of the group that night were suffering problems in their personal life and none of us wanted to burden the group with those problems. But by trying to keep those problems to ourselves, it affected what we were able to achieve Spiritually together.

At the end of the evening, Sojah presented the following cleansing meditation to us, as an attempt to clear some elements of our problems and raise our energy together. We all felt a lot better afterwards and there was much sharing that brought us closer.

Here is an adaptation of this cleansing meditation that could be useful at times when you need help to clear inner blockages and open the Spiritual channels:

*Place yourself in a comfortable position in a situation where you can relax with little likelihood that you will be disturbed. Close your eyes, and once more, focus upon your breathing, letting the rhythm of your breathing become steadier, so it just slows down a little, and you feel yourself start to go within.*

*Imagine as if there is a wave of relaxation spreading through your body, letting your body become heavier and heavier, so it is almost as if it is not there. Just continue being aware of your breath as you go deeper and deeper within. Then, as you no longer need to bother about your physical body, you start to feel lighter. There could be a feeling of swaying, just slightly swaying, as you begin to rise upwards. You feel more and more light and with your awareness, you are lifting up, up towards the light. It is a wonderful feeling and you welcome this. It is as though you are energy and you are free. There is bright light, and you slowly move towards it. You know that this is where you need to go. As you rise towards it, the light slowly comes towards you, and it becomes brighter and warmer, and engulfs you. With your journey, you now pass right into this light. Your consciousness is adjusting, and you pass right through this light, and then emerges on the other side.*

*Now in your vision, and your sense of location, I would like to suggest that you are on top of a mountain. The atmosphere is rich and clear, and below you on your left, you become aware of a beautiful forest of pines, and also a beautiful beach. The beach and the sea next to it are enticing you today, and you feel very drawn there. As you allow this thought, you find that you are traveling downwards, drifting gently backwards and forwards along the beach.*

*Soon you feel the beautiful warm sensation of the sand beneath your feet. You are standing on the beach, and there close by you, is your guide. You may sense or see the presence of your guide, and you feel the quality of their love, and you know that you are safe.*

*In front of you is the sea; it is a wonderful ocean, full of power and vitality. Here, in the Spiritual realm, you do not need to be afraid. This sea can do you no harm, it cannot drown you, and it cannot make you short of breath. It is there for you to enjoy and embrace.*

*Today, you will go into the sea. Your guide is with you, and you feel the strength to go forward. Slowly you advance into the water. You feel comfortable and at ease. There is a feeling of excitement, connecting with the energy of this vast ocean.*

*Now there are waves, and you are aware of a large one that is approaching. This wave is going to hit you and cascade over you. You stand steady and the wave comes. As it pushes against you, and you feel it cleansing you. It washes away from you all the doubts that you have had in your mind, and as the wave moves on, there is the feeling that the water has taken with it all the doubts that you were carrying, and now you believe, and you have more clarity and faith than you have had for a long time. You are aware of your guide with you and feel very close and contented.*

*(Pause)*

*There is a second wave now approaching in the distance. This one is stronger, because it wants to wash away bitterness and anger that has been in you. Bitterness and anger can affect the balance and energetic workings of your body. It can bring about chemical reactions that result in illness ultimately. Everyone does get angry at times, although it is not so much the anger as the bitterness that is harboured. And this is something that you do not need.*

*This wave, then, as it rolls towards you, is coming to help you, to wash away any bitterness that you have there, and to enable you to gain a greater perspective. And to realize that whatever you have been holding inside you is not worth it. It is not worth being ill for, and it is not worth harbouring inside you. So if you can, as this wave reaches you now, let it wash that bitterness away.*

*(Pause)*

*Now there is a third wave approaching you. This one feels different to the others. There is an atmosphere of joy about it. This wave is bringing love. You know that you need love, and you welcome this energy that is swiftly coming towards you. As it rises above you and washes down upon you, you feel all the power and love and energy. You feel this energy absorb itself into you, and you feel free. You want to join in with this sea and dive into the waves. There is silkiness and warmth and you feel held and supported by the sea. There is goodness in this sea, and more and more, you feel at one with it.*

*If you have been carrying any worries or troubles, you can now quietly say them to yourself, and then feel the waves wash over you and gently clear those away. Just find yourself doing that now. It is pleasant, comfortable and very helpful.*

*(Long Pause)*

*When you are ready, you can come out of the sea and for a few minutes, sit down on the beach. Your guide is there with you, but you may also like to think about someone that you love or care about, and try to feel their presence, if only for a few moments. Know that they are with you, sharing your experience of this beautiful place. Take some time to do that now.*

*(Pause)*

*You can come here any time. The Spiritual realm is your home. You have only to close your eyes as you are doing now, and in your own way, if you wish, meditate and bring yourself to this cleansing sea, and can feel the benefit of this.*

*But now, sadly, it is time to leave this, so, when you are ready, slowly rise up from the beach. Bring with you the memory and feeling of the sea so in doing this, you can feel lighter in having shed some of your problems. With your guide, you know you will remain connected.*

*Slowly you enter back into your physical body. You do this gently and gradually, feeling your limbs and the sensation of moving your body again. You wait until your conscious feels normal again, and only then, slowly open your eyes, with a feeling of well-being and gratitude for what you have experienced.*

### The Golden River Meditation

The final meditation that I would like to include is one that Sojah used many times with us in our healing group. It is guided through quite specific imagery that can help us learn what it is like in the Summerland and what we can expect there. We are introduced to the beauty and wonder of the Spiritual world in a way so that it becomes familiar to us, and our Earthly consciousness feels that we can be there.

In the Spiritual realm, we are free to use thought as our means of transportation and communication with other beings and energies that are there. The meditation incorporates this notion and allows us to experiment with utilizing thought through our own inner experience.

Central to the meditation is the concept that the Summerland is a very loving and joyful place where we can express our selves freely and there are endless possibilities and potentials for how we can be. Our guides are close to us if we need them, and through their help, we can learn and grow.

Here is the meditation we have called 'The Golden River Meditation':

*To start this meditation, be in that comfortable place where you can be quiet and where you are not likely to be disturbed. Sit or lie down comfortably, as you prefer, and close your eyes. Let yourself begin to relax. Then, as we usually do, become aware of the rhythm of your breathing and focus on that. Let your breathing settle and become more and more regular as you find yourself drifting deeper and deeper within.*

*With your breathing helping you to go within, also imagine your body relaxing, just becoming heavier and more and more droopy so you don't need to be bothered with it any more.*

*As you go deeper now, let us invoke the light and love of Spirit to be with you, so you imagine that with every breath, you are drawing that Spiritual energy closer into your being. Just imagine that there is a light that surrounds you. It is warm and energetic, so as you adjust, you feel comfortable with it. If you do not see it, sense it as if it is there. There could be a colour that you resonate with. Imagine this around you, keeping you snug and warm, so you feel very restful. You are safe and protected and prepared for a wonderful experience to unfold.*

*Let us now work with the third eye. As you become even more relaxed, you become aware of the centre of your forehead, because this is where you use your third eye. Imagine now, very slowly, that you are opening this eye, like opening a curtain, and in front of you, there is a door.*

*Check within you that you are ready to proceed, and if so, open this door now. As you do so, a wonderful, warm light meets you. There is also a very light breeze. With your third eye, you can look or sense what is around you, and I would like to suggest that there about you is a beautiful meadow. Open your senses to the beauty of this place. The colours are rich and intensely powerful. You feel quite emotionally affected being here. It is a feeling of being happy and free.*

*As you become aware of more of the details of this scene, you may notice other Spiritual beings that are there. They could appear as streams of light, or you might sense them as having specific forms that you can recognize to distinguish one from the other. You feel welcomed and able to proceed on your journey.*

*As you gaze across the meadow, you notice that beyond that, there is a pathway that leads down over a mountain. Let us go this way today. You notice trees and other vegetation that is there, and all the nature has a vibrant energy about it that is very uplifting and satisfying.*

*The air also feels alive, and I wish to suggest that it has the feeling of being a warm summer evening, just the right temperature so that you feel relaxed and contented*

*Now you reach the end of this track, and you are at the top of the mountain overlooking a deep valley below you. Looking down, at the base of this valley is a majestic, winding river. You feel the energy of this river, and feel very attracted to it. There is the feeling inside you that you would like to go there.*

*In the Spiritual realm you travel through the generation of your thoughts. So there could be a number of ways that you could travel to the river. One route could be for you to jump off the side of the mountain and allow yourself to float downwards, just knowing that you are now in a place where you cannot be harmed, and so much is possible. Otherwise, you can also express the wish clearly inside your mind that you are by the river, and then you are there. So, by whatever means you want to use, just come down to the river now.*

*And here we are, by the river. It is flowing smoothly, and the sun is shining on this, causing an almost golden light. Again, you feel its energy. You are sitting now on a grassy bank, which is also pulsing with energy. And you are feeling very comfortable.*

*If you wish, you can swim in the river. You can swim for as long as you wish, and when you step out, you will not be wet. The moisture will immediately evaporate, and you will be dry, because this is a different dimension. The form of things here is much more fluid and in motion. If you were to try to eat fruit here, you would feel the sensations of the juices, and could enjoy the taste, as if you were really eating it, but then the energy of the fruit would dissolve because you do not need physical food here.*

*So as you are here by the river, you can explore and express what you desire to do. You can swim or watch the surrounding, and let yourself play, whatever you choose.*

(Long pause)

*It is possible you may wish for companionship. There could be someone by your side, your Spiritual guide, or even someone who you have loved that has passed into Spirit, or perhaps even the Higher Self of someone that you know on Earth. You can share this space with that other being, and do what you wish together. In your mind, it is possible that you can talk together, and have dialogue. This may be an opportunity to gain help for any problems that have been bothering you. In this wonderful environment, much will be clearer for you, and you can learn more deeply about some aspect of your life, or just relax, if you prefer.*

*If it is your guide that is there, they may like to show you a vision or offer help to you if there is some particular challenge that you are facing as a soul. They will only offer help if you want it, so you feel at ease, knowing that the choice is with you.*

*Whatever you learn here will stay with you, so that when you return to your physical body, you will really know that you have been conversing with Spirit.*

*So now you take that time to relate with your Spiritual friends, and whatever you need to do and share together.*

*(Long pause)*

*Slowly now you can complete the experience that you have been having. This journey is one that you can practice. Coming to the golden river can be a starting point and a foundation, if you feel comfortable with it, from which you can then engage with further explorations.*

*Soon we will return from this wonderful Spiritual journey. You will probably feel very refreshed and well rested from the experience, and also more knowledgeable about Spirit.*

*So now, find that you are rising up from the river side, and you are returning gradually to your physical body, just returning the way you have come, closing the door behind you, and allowing your third eye to resume its normal function. With all that you have invoked and the Spiritual support, you can give thanks and allow those to dissolve and return to source.*

*Now, become aware again of the weight of your physical body. Feel that you can move your limbs, and gently test that you are fully connected to your physical body. Then very gradually, only when you feel that you have fully returned, you can open your eyes.*

*The experience you have had will be with you, and it may be of benefit if you can spend a little time to write it down, so you can honour it, just like you would if it had been a dream.*

*Thank you for listening.*

# *Moving On*

Four years on from Marjorie's death, Reg still speaks to her every day, as if she was there with him. Marjorie's soul journey continues in a form that I no longer can reach with my normal consciousness. I would speculate that she will be around and very close when Reg passes on and that they will be very happy to be reunited.

Through her Spiritual work, Marjorie's soul has shone a light on the journey that we are to travel as souls. In her humanness and vulnerability, she has highlighted trials and challenges that we all must meet to rise higher and go further in our development. In the teachings of her guide, Sojah, she has left a legacy of insight and inner pathways to explore. In the way that she approached her Spiritual service, her dedication and humility, even with the limitations she struggled with, it is a model to inspire.

There are winds of change in the consciousness of humanity. The doorway between our human consciousness and the Spiritual worlds is being opened. Marjorie has been one of those pioneers to show us how it could be done and what could be achieved. Now it is up to us to make our own steps so we can be connected with our true nature as souls and with the Spiritual worlds of love.

# *Contact*

Paul offers a range of professional services including individual therapy sessions, workshops, classes, talks and Spiritual support.

Paul Williamson
www.paulwilliamson.co.uk
pgwilliamson@hotmail.co.uk
Mobile: 07948215333

Published by Soul Light Publishing

Printed by Baytypesetters (01524) 850056